C-3727   CAREER EXAMINATION SERIES

This is your
PASSBOOK for...

Junior Accountant

Test Preparation Study Guide
Questions & Answers

COPYRIGHT NOTICE

This book is SOLELY intended for, is sold ONLY to, and its use is RESTRICTED to individual, bona fide applicants or candidates who qualify by virtue of having seriously filed applications for appropriate license, certificate, professional and/or promotional advancement, higher school matriculation, scholarship, or other legitimate requirements of education and/or governmental authorities.

This book is NOT intended for use, class instruction, tutoring, training, duplication, copying, reprinting, excerption, or adaptation, etc., by:

1) Other publishers
2) Proprietors and/or Instructors of "Coaching" and/or Preparatory Courses
3) Personnel and/or Training Divisions of commercial, industrial, and governmental organizations
4) Schools, colleges, or universities and/or their departments and staffs, including teachers and other personnel
5) Testing Agencies or Bureaus
6) Study groups which seek by the purchase of a single volume to copy and/or duplicate and/or adapt this material for use by the group as a whole without having purchased individual volumes for each of the members of the group
7) Et al.

Such persons would be in violation of appropriate Federal and State statutes.

PROVISION OF LICENSING AGREEMENTS – Recognized educational, commercial, industrial, and governmental institutions and organizations, and others legitimately engaged in educational pursuits, including training, testing, and measurement activities, may address request for a licensing agreement to the copyright owners, who will determine whether, and under what conditions, including fees and charges, the materials in this book may be used them. In other words, a licensing facility exists for the legitimate use of the material in this book on other than an individual basis. However, it is asseverated and affirmed here that the material in this book CANNOT be used without the receipt of the express permission of such a licensing agreement from the Publishers. Inquiries re licensing should be addressed to the company, attention rights and permissions department.

All rights reserved, including the right of reproduction in whole or in part, in any form or by any means, electronic or mechanical, including photocopying, recording, or by any information storage and retrieval system, without permission in writing from the Publisher.

Copyright © 2024 by
National Learning Corporation

212 Michael Drive, Syosset, NY 11791
(516) 921-8888 • www.passbooks.com
E-mail: info@passbooks.com

PASSBOOK® SERIES

THE *PASSBOOK® SERIES* has been created to prepare applicants and candidates for the ultimate academic battlefield – the examination room.

At some time in our lives, each and every one of us may be required to take an examination – for validation, matriculation, admission, qualification, registration, certification, or licensure.

Based on the assumption that every applicant or candidate has met the basic formal educational standards, has taken the required number of courses, and read the necessary texts, the *PASSBOOK® SERIES* furnishes the one special preparation which may assure passing with confidence, instead of failing with insecurity. Examination questions – together with answers – are furnished as the basic vehicle for study so that the mysteries of the examination and its compounding difficulties may be eliminated or diminished by a sure method.

This book is meant to help you pass your examination provided that you qualify and are serious in your objective.

The entire field is reviewed through the huge store of content information which is succinctly presented through a provocative and challenging approach – the question-and-answer method.

A climate of success is established by furnishing the correct answers at the end of each test.

You soon learn to recognize types of questions, forms of questions, and patterns of questioning. You may even begin to anticipate expected outcomes.

You perceive that many questions are repeated or adapted so that you can gain acute insights, which may enable you to score many sure points.

You learn how to confront new questions, or types of questions, and to attack them confidently and work out the correct answers.

You note objectives and emphases, and recognize pitfalls and dangers, so that you may make positive educational adjustments.

Moreover, you are kept fully informed in relation to new concepts, methods, practices, and directions in the field.

You discover that you are actually taking the examination all the time: you are preparing for the examination by "taking" an examination, not by reading extraneous and/or supererogatory textbooks.

In short, this PASSBOOK®, used directedly, should be an important factor in helping you to pass your test.

JUNIOR ACCOUNANT

DUTIES:
Under the general supervision of a higher level position, an incumbent of this class performs moderately complex accounting and auditing work including the preparation of financial statements and analyses, in accordance with standard professional accounting procedures. Incumbents maintain financial records either manually or by using various computer applications and programs. This position is distinguished from that of Accountant in that it is an entry-level position and does not perform the same level of varied and complex assignments as assigned to the Accountant. The incumbent may act as lead worker and/or give technical assistance to other personnel. Assists in the performance of general accounting duties such as maintaining a general ledger, making journal entries, determining fund balances, taking trial balances and reconciling bank accounts; performs preliminary work necessary for the development or refinement of accounting systems; may supervise the preparation of payroll; assists in the pre-audit of accounts to ensure proper expenditure control. Does related work as required.

SUBJECT OF EXAMINATION:
A written test designed to evaluate knowledge, skills and /or abilities in the following areas:
1. **General accounting** - These questions test for knowledge of the general accounting principles a d practices used in the preparation of financial statements, in the recording and reporting of financial transactions, and in financial decision-making. Candidates will be required to demonstrate a current knowledge of Generally Accepted Accounting Principles (GAAP). Knowledge of computerized information systems as it applies to accounting may be required.
2. **General auditing** - These questions test for knowledge of the principles and procedures involve I in substantiating and examining transactions and financial statements. It will require a knowledge of auditing techniques and Generally Accepted Auditing Standards (GAAS). Knowledge of the use of computerized accounting or auditing systems as it pertains to auditing may be required. Questions relating to internal controls applicable to manual and computerized accounting systems may be included.
3. **Preparing written material** - These questions test for the ability to present information clearly and accurately, and to organize paragraphs logically and comprehensibly. For some questions, you will be given information in two or three sentences followed by four restatements of the Information. You must then choose the best version. For other questions, you will be given paragraphs with their sentences out of order. You must then choose, from four suggestions, the best order for the sentences.
4. **Understanding and interpreting tabular material** - These questions test your ability to understand, analyze, and use the internal logic of data presented in tabular form. You may be asked to perform tasks such as completing tables, drawing conclusions from them, analyzing data trends or interrelationships, and revising or combining data sets. The concepts of rate, ratio, and proportion are tested. Mathematical operations are simple, and computational speed is not a major factor in the test.

HOW TO TAKE A TEST

I. YOU MUST PASS AN EXAMINATION

A. WHAT EVERY CANDIDATE SHOULD KNOW

Examination applicants often ask us for help in preparing for the written test. What can I study in advance? What kinds of questions will be asked? How will the test be given? How will the papers be graded?

As an applicant for a civil service examination, you may be wondering about some of these things. Our purpose here is to suggest effective methods of advance study and to describe civil service examinations.

Your chances for success on this examination can be increased if you know how to prepare. Those "pre-examination jitters" can be reduced if you know what to expect. You can even experience an adventure in good citizenship if you know why civil service exams are given.

B. WHY ARE CIVIL SERVICE EXAMINATIONS GIVEN?

Civil service examinations are important to you in two ways. As a citizen, you want public jobs filled by employees who know how to do their work. As a job seeker, you want a fair chance to compete for that job on an equal footing with other candidates. The best-known means of accomplishing this two-fold goal is the competitive examination.

Exams are widely publicized throughout the nation. They may be administered for jobs in federal, state, city, municipal, town or village governments or agencies.

Any citizen may apply, with some limitations, such as the age or residence of applicants. Your experience and education may be reviewed to see whether you meet the requirements for the particular examination. When these requirements exist, they are reasonable and applied consistently to all applicants. Thus, a competitive examination may cause you some uneasiness now, but it is your privilege and safeguard.

C. HOW ARE CIVIL SERVICE EXAMS DEVELOPED?

Examinations are carefully written by trained technicians who are specialists in the field known as "psychological measurement," in consultation with recognized authorities in the field of work that the test will cover. These experts recommend the subject matter areas or skills to be tested; only those knowledges or skills important to your success on the job are included. The most reliable books and source materials available are used as references. Together, the experts and technicians judge the difficulty level of the questions.

Test technicians know how to phrase questions so that the problem is clearly stated. Their ethics do not permit "trick" or "catch" questions. Questions may have been tried out on sample groups, or subjected to statistical analysis, to determine their usefulness.

Written tests are often used in combination with performance tests, ratings of training and experience, and oral interviews. All of these measures combine to form the best-known means of finding the right person for the right job.

II. HOW TO PASS THE WRITTEN TEST

A. NATURE OF THE EXAMINATION

To prepare intelligently for civil service examinations, you should know how they differ from school examinations you have taken. In school you were assigned certain definite pages to read or subjects to cover. The examination questions were quite detailed and usually emphasized memory. Civil service exams, on the other hand, try to discover your present ability to perform the duties of a position, plus your potentiality to learn these duties. In other words, a civil service exam attempts to predict how successful you will be. Questions cover such a broad area that they cannot be as minute and detailed as school exam questions.

In the public service similar kinds of work, or positions, are grouped together in one "class." This process is known as *position-classification*. All the positions in a class are paid according to the salary range for that class. One class title covers all of these positions, and they are all tested by the same examination.

B. FOUR BASIC STEPS

1) Study the announcement

How, then, can you know what subjects to study? Our best answer is: "Learn as much as possible about the class of positions for which you've applied." The exam will test the knowledge, skills and abilities needed to do the work.

Your most valuable source of information about the position you want is the official exam announcement. This announcement lists the training and experience qualifications. Check these standards and apply only if you come reasonably close to meeting them.

The brief description of the position in the examination announcement offers some clues to the subjects which will be tested. Think about the job itself. Review the duties in your mind. Can you perform them, or are there some in which you are rusty? Fill in the blank spots in your preparation.

Many jurisdictions preview the written test in the exam announcement by including a section called "Knowledge and Abilities Required," "Scope of the Examination," or some similar heading. Here you will find out specifically what fields will be tested.

2) Review your own background

Once you learn in general what the position is all about, and what you need to know to do the work, ask yourself which subjects you already know fairly well and which need improvement. You may wonder whether to concentrate on improving your strong areas or on building some background in your fields of weakness. When the announcement has specified "some knowledge" or "considerable knowledge," or has used adjectives like "beginning principles of..." or "advanced ... methods," you can get a clue as to the number and difficulty of questions to be asked in any given field. More questions, and hence broader coverage, would be included for those subjects which are more important in the work. Now weigh your strengths and weaknesses against the job requirements and prepare accordingly.

3) Determine the level of the position

Another way to tell how intensively you should prepare is to understand the level of the job for which you are applying. Is it the entering level? In other words, is this the position in which beginners in a field of work are hired? Or is it an intermediate or advanced level? Sometimes this is indicated by such words as "Junior" or "Senior" in the class title. Other jurisdictions use Roman numerals to designate the level – Clerk I, Clerk II, for example. The word "Supervisor" sometimes appears in the title. If the level is not indicated by the title, check the description of duties. Will you be working under very close supervision, or will you have responsibility for independent decisions in this work?

4) Choose appropriate study materials

Now that you know the subjects to be examined and the relative amount of each subject to be covered, you can choose suitable study materials. For beginning level jobs, or even advanced ones, if you have a pronounced weakness in some aspect of your training, read a modern, standard textbook in that field. Be sure it is up to date and has general coverage. Such books are normally available at your library, and the librarian will be glad to help you locate one. For entry-level positions, questions of appropriate difficulty are chosen – neither highly advanced questions, nor those too simple. Such questions require careful thought but not advanced training.

If the position for which you are applying is technical or advanced, you will read more advanced, specialized material. If you are already familiar with the basic principles of your field, elementary textbooks would waste your time. Concentrate on advanced textbooks and technical periodicals. Think through the concepts and review difficult problems in your field.

These are all general sources. You can get more ideas on your own initiative, following these leads. For example, training manuals and publications of the government agency which employs workers in your field can be useful, particularly for technical and professional positions. A letter or visit to the government department involved may result in more specific study suggestions, and certainly will provide you with a more definite idea of the exact nature of the position you are seeking.

III. KINDS OF TESTS

Tests are used for purposes other than measuring knowledge and ability to perform specified duties. For some positions, it is equally important to test ability to make adjustments to new situations or to profit from training. In others, basic mental abilities not dependent on information are essential. Questions which test these things may not appear as pertinent to the duties of the position as those which test for knowledge and information. Yet they are often highly important parts of a fair examination. For very general questions, it is almost impossible to help you direct your study efforts. What we can do is to point out some of the more common of these general abilities needed in public service positions and describe some typical questions.

1) General information

Broad, general information has been found useful for predicting job success in some kinds of work. This is tested in a variety of ways, from vocabulary lists to questions about current events. Basic background in some field of work, such as sociology or economics, may be sampled in a group of questions. Often these are principles which have become familiar to most persons through exposure rather than through formal training. It is difficult to advise you how to study for these questions; being alert to the world around you is our best suggestion.

2) Verbal ability

An example of an ability needed in many positions is verbal or language ability. Verbal ability is, in brief, the ability to use and understand words. Vocabulary and grammar tests are typical measures of this ability. Reading comprehension or paragraph interpretation questions are common in many kinds of civil service tests. You are given a paragraph of written material and asked to find its central meaning.

3) Numerical ability

Number skills can be tested by the familiar arithmetic problem, by checking paired lists of numbers to see which are alike and which are different, or by interpreting charts and graphs. In the latter test, a graph may be printed in the test booklet which you are asked to use as the basis for answering questions.

4) Observation

A popular test for law-enforcement positions is the observation test. A picture is shown to you for several minutes, then taken away. Questions about the picture test your ability to observe both details and larger elements.

5) Following directions

In many positions in the public service, the employee must be able to carry out written instructions dependably and accurately. You may be given a chart with several columns, each column listing a variety of information. The questions require you to carry out directions involving the information given in the chart.

6) Skills and aptitudes

Performance tests effectively measure some manual skills and aptitudes. When the skill is one in which you are trained, such as typing or shorthand, you can practice. These tests are often very much like those given in business school or high school courses. For many of the other skills and aptitudes, however, no short-time preparation can be made. Skills and abilities natural to you or that you have developed throughout your lifetime are being tested.

Many of the general questions just described provide all the data needed to answer the questions and ask you to use your reasoning ability to find the answers. Your best preparation for these tests, as well as for tests of facts and ideas, is to be at your physical and mental best. You, no doubt, have your own methods of getting into an exam-taking mood and keeping "in shape." The next section lists some ideas on this subject.

IV. KINDS OF QUESTIONS

Only rarely is the "essay" question, which you answer in narrative form, used in civil service tests. Civil service tests are usually of the short-answer type. Full instructions for answering these questions will be given to you at the examination. But in case this is your first experience with short-answer questions and separate answer sheets, here is what you need to know:

1) Multiple-choice Questions

Most popular of the short-answer questions is the "multiple choice" or "best answer" question. It can be used, for example, to test for factual knowledge, ability to solve problems or judgment in meeting situations found at work.

A multiple-choice question is normally one of three types—
- It can begin with an incomplete statement followed by several possible endings. You are to find the one ending which *best* completes the statement, although some of the others may not be entirely wrong.
- It can also be a complete statement in the form of a question which is answered by choosing one of the statements listed.

- It can be in the form of a problem – again you select the best answer.

Here is an example of a multiple-choice question with a discussion which should give you some clues as to the method for choosing the right answer:

When an employee has a complaint about his assignment, the action which will *best* help him overcome his difficulty is to
- A. discuss his difficulty with his coworkers
- B. take the problem to the head of the organization
- C. take the problem to the person who gave him the assignment
- D. say nothing to anyone about his complaint

In answering this question, you should study each of the choices to find which is best. Consider choice "A" – Certainly an employee may discuss his complaint with fellow employees, but no change or improvement can result, and the complaint remains unresolved. Choice "B" is a poor choice since the head of the organization probably does not know what assignment you have been given, and taking your problem to him is known as "going over the head" of the supervisor. The supervisor, or person who made the assignment, is the person who can clarify it or correct any injustice. Choice "C" is, therefore, correct. To say nothing, as in choice "D," is unwise. Supervisors have and interest in knowing the problems employees are facing, and the employee is seeking a solution to his problem.

2) True/False Questions

The "true/false" or "right/wrong" form of question is sometimes used. Here a complete statement is given. Your job is to decide whether the statement is right or wrong.

SAMPLE: A roaming cell-phone call to a nearby city costs less than a non-roaming call to a distant city.

This statement is wrong, or false, since roaming calls are more expensive.

This is not a complete list of all possible question forms, although most of the others are variations of these common types. You will always get complete directions for answering questions. Be sure you understand *how* to mark your answers – ask questions until you do.

V. RECORDING YOUR ANSWERS

Computer terminals are used more and more today for many different kinds of exams.

For an examination with very few applicants, you may be told to record your answers in the test booklet itself. Separate answer sheets are much more common. If this separate answer sheet is to be scored by machine – and this is often the case – it is highly important that you mark your answers correctly in order to get credit.

An electronic scoring machine is often used in civil service offices because of the speed with which papers can be scored. Machine-scored answer sheets must be marked with a pencil, which will be given to you. This pencil has a high graphite content which responds to the electronic scoring machine. As a matter of fact, stray dots may register as answers, so do not let your pencil rest on the answer sheet while you are pondering the correct answer. Also, if your pencil lead breaks or is otherwise defective, ask for another.

Since the answer sheet will be dropped in a slot in the scoring machine, be careful not to bend the corners or get the paper crumpled.

The answer sheet normally has five vertical columns of numbers, with 30 numbers to a column. These numbers correspond to the question numbers in your test booklet. After each number, going across the page are four or five pairs of dotted lines. These short dotted lines have small letters or numbers above them. The first two pairs may also have a "T" or "F" above the letters. This indicates that the first two pairs only are to be used if the questions are of the true-false type. If the questions are multiple choice, disregard the "T" and "F" and pay attention only to the small letters or numbers.

Answer your questions in the manner of the sample that follows:

32. The largest city in the United States is
    A. Washington, D.C.
    B. New York City
    C. Chicago
    D. Detroit
    E. San Francisco

1) Choose the answer you think is best. (New York City is the largest, so "B" is correct.)
2) Find the row of dotted lines numbered the same as the question you are answering. (Find row number 32)
3) Find the pair of dotted lines corresponding to the answer. (Find the pair of lines under the mark "B.")
4) Make a solid black mark between the dotted lines.

VI. BEFORE THE TEST

Common sense will help you find procedures to follow to get ready for an examination. Too many of us, however, overlook these sensible measures. Indeed, nervousness and fatigue have been found to be the most serious reasons why applicants fail to do their best on civil service tests. Here is a list of reminders:

- Begin your preparation early – Don't wait until the last minute to go scurrying around for books and materials or to find out what the position is all about.
- Prepare continuously – An hour a night for a week is better than an all-night cram session. This has been definitely established. What is more, a night a week for a month will return better dividends than crowding your study into a shorter period of time.
- Locate the place of the exam – You have been sent a notice telling you when and where to report for the examination. If the location is in a different town or otherwise unfamiliar to you, it would be well to inquire the best route and learn something about the building.
- Relax the night before the test – Allow your mind to rest. Do not study at all that night. Plan some mild recreation or diversion; then go to bed early and get a good night's sleep.
- Get up early enough to make a leisurely trip to the place for the test – This way unforeseen events, traffic snarls, unfamiliar buildings, etc. will not upset you.
- Dress comfortably – A written test is not a fashion show. You will be known by number and not by name, so wear something comfortable.

- Leave excess paraphernalia at home – Shopping bags and odd bundles will get in your way. You need bring only the items mentioned in the official notice you received; usually everything you need is provided. Do not bring reference books to the exam. They will only confuse those last minutes and be taken away from you when in the test room.
- Arrive somewhat ahead of time – If because of transportation schedules you must get there very early, bring a newspaper or magazine to take your mind off yourself while waiting.
- Locate the examination room – When you have found the proper room, you will be directed to the seat or part of the room where you will sit. Sometimes you are given a sheet of instructions to read while you are waiting. Do not fill out any forms until you are told to do so; just read them and be prepared.
- Relax and prepare to listen to the instructions
- If you have any physical problem that may keep you from doing your best, be sure to tell the test administrator. If you are sick or in poor health, you really cannot do your best on the exam. You can come back and take the test some other time.

VII. AT THE TEST

The day of the test is here and you have the test booklet in your hand. The temptation to get going is very strong. Caution! There is more to success than knowing the right answers. You must know how to identify your papers and understand variations in the type of short-answer question used in this particular examination. Follow these suggestions for maximum results from your efforts:

1) Cooperate with the monitor

The test administrator has a duty to create a situation in which you can be as much at ease as possible. He will give instructions, tell you when to begin, check to see that you are marking your answer sheet correctly, and so on. He is not there to guard you, although he will see that your competitors do not take unfair advantage. He wants to help you do your best.

2) Listen to all instructions

Don't jump the gun! Wait until you understand all directions. In most civil service tests you get more time than you need to answer the questions. So don't be in a hurry. Read each word of instructions until you clearly understand the meaning. Study the examples, listen to all announcements and follow directions. Ask questions if you do not understand what to do.

3) Identify your papers

Civil service exams are usually identified by number only. You will be assigned a number; you must not put your name on your test papers. Be sure to copy your number correctly. Since more than one exam may be given, copy your exact examination title.

4) Plan your time

Unless you are told that a test is a "speed" or "rate of work" test, speed itself is usually not important. Time enough to answer all the questions will be provided, but this does not mean that you have all day. An overall time limit has been set. Divide the total time (in minutes) by the number of questions to determine the approximate time you have for each question.

5) Do not linger over difficult questions

If you come across a difficult question, mark it with a paper clip (useful to have along) and come back to it when you have been through the booklet. One caution if you do this – be sure to skip a number on your answer sheet as well. Check often to be sure that you have not lost your place and that you are marking in the row numbered the same as the question you are answering.

6) Read the questions

Be sure you know what the question asks! Many capable people are unsuccessful because they failed to *read* the questions correctly.

7) Answer all questions

Unless you have been instructed that a penalty will be deducted for incorrect answers, it is better to guess than to omit a question.

8) Speed tests

It is often better NOT to guess on speed tests. It has been found that on timed tests people are tempted to spend the last few seconds before time is called in marking answers at random – without even reading them – in the hope of picking up a few extra points. To discourage this practice, the instructions may warn you that your score will be "corrected" for guessing. That is, a penalty will be applied. The incorrect answers will be deducted from the correct ones, or some other penalty formula will be used.

9) Review your answers

If you finish before time is called, go back to the questions you guessed or omitted to give them further thought. Review other answers if you have time.

10) Return your test materials

If you are ready to leave before others have finished or time is called, take ALL your materials to the monitor and leave quietly. Never take any test material with you. The monitor can discover whose papers are not complete, and taking a test booklet may be grounds for disqualification.

VIII. EXAMINATION TECHNIQUES

1) Read the general instructions carefully. These are usually printed on the first page of the exam booklet. As a rule, these instructions refer to the timing of the examination; the fact that you should not start work until the signal and must stop work at a signal, etc. If there are any *special* instructions, such as a choice of questions to be answered, make sure that you note this instruction carefully.

2) When you are ready to start work on the examination, that is as soon as the signal has been given, read the instructions to each question booklet, underline any key words or phrases, such as *least, best, outline, describe* and the like. In this way you will tend to answer as requested rather than discover on reviewing your paper that you *listed without describing*, that you selected the *worst* choice rather than the *best* choice, etc.

3) If the examination is of the objective or multiple-choice type – that is, each question will also give a series of possible answers: A, B, C or D, and you are called upon to select the best answer and write the letter next to that answer on your answer paper – it is advisable to start answering each question in turn. There may be anywhere from 50 to 100 such questions in the three or four hours allotted and you can see how much time would be taken if you read through all the questions before beginning to answer any. Furthermore, if you come across a question or group of questions which you know would be difficult to answer, it would undoubtedly affect your handling of all the other questions.

4) If the examination is of the essay type and contains but a few questions, it is a moot point as to whether you should read all the questions before starting to answer any one. Of course, if you are given a choice – say five out of seven and the like – then it is essential to read all the questions so you can eliminate the two that are most difficult. If, however, you are asked to answer all the questions, there may be danger in trying to answer the easiest one first because you may find that you will spend too much time on it. The best technique is to answer the first question, then proceed to the second, etc.

5) Time your answers. Before the exam begins, write down the time it started, then add the time allowed for the examination and write down the time it must be completed, then divide the time available somewhat as follows:
    - If 3-1/2 hours are allowed, that would be 210 minutes. If you have 80 objective-type questions, that would be an average of 2-1/2 minutes per question. Allow yourself no more than 2 minutes per question, or a total of 160 minutes, which will permit about 50 minutes to review.
    - If for the time allotment of 210 minutes there are 7 essay questions to answer, that would average about 30 minutes a question. Give yourself only 25 minutes per question so that you have about 35 minutes to review.

6) The most important instruction is to *read each question* and make sure you know what is wanted. The second most important instruction is to *time yourself properly* so that you answer every question. The third most important instruction is to *answer every question*. Guess if you have to but include something for each question. Remember that you will receive no credit for a blank and will probably receive some credit if you write something in answer to an essay question. If you guess a letter – say "B" for a multiple-choice question – you may have guessed right. If you leave a blank as an answer to a multiple-choice question, the examiners may respect your feelings but it will not add a point to your score. Some exams may penalize you for wrong answers, so in such cases *only*, you may not want to guess unless you have some basis for your answer.

7) Suggestions
    a. Objective-type questions
        1. Examine the question booklet for proper sequence of pages and questions
        2. Read all instructions carefully
        3. Skip any question which seems too difficult; return to it after all other questions have been answered
        4. Apportion your time properly; do not spend too much time on any single question or group of questions

5. Note and underline key words – *all, most, fewest, least, best, worst, same, opposite,* etc.
6. Pay particular attention to negatives
7. Note unusual option, e.g., unduly long, short, complex, different or similar in content to the body of the question
8. Observe the use of "hedging" words – *probably, may, most likely,* etc.
9. Make sure that your answer is put next to the same number as the question
10. Do not second-guess unless you have good reason to believe the second answer is definitely more correct
11. Cross out original answer if you decide another answer is more accurate; do not erase until you are ready to hand your paper in
12. Answer all questions; guess unless instructed otherwise
13. Leave time for review

  b. Essay questions
   1. Read each question carefully
   2. Determine exactly what is wanted. Underline key words or phrases.
   3. Decide on outline or paragraph answer
   4. Include many different points and elements unless asked to develop any one or two points or elements
   5. Show impartiality by giving pros and cons unless directed to select one side only
   6. Make and write down any assumptions you find necessary to answer the questions
   7. Watch your English, grammar, punctuation and choice of words
   8. Time your answers; don't crowd material

8) Answering the essay question

Most essay questions can be answered by framing the specific response around several key words or ideas. Here are a few such key words or ideas:

M's: manpower, materials, methods, money, management
P's: purpose, program, policy, plan, procedure, practice, problems, pitfalls, personnel, public relations

  a. Six basic steps in handling problems:
   1. Preliminary plan and background development
   2. Collect information, data and facts
   3. Analyze and interpret information, data and facts
   4. Analyze and develop solutions as well as make recommendations
   5. Prepare report and sell recommendations
   6. Install recommendations and follow up effectiveness

  b. Pitfalls to avoid
   1. *Taking things for granted* – A statement of the situation does not necessarily imply that each of the elements is necessarily true; for example, a complaint may be invalid and biased so that all that can be taken for granted is that a complaint has been registered

2. *Considering only one side of a situation* – Wherever possible, indicate several alternatives and then point out the reasons you selected the best one
3. *Failing to indicate follow up* – Whenever your answer indicates action on your part, make certain that you will take proper follow-up action to see how successful your recommendations, procedures or actions turn out to be
4. *Taking too long in answering any single question* – Remember to time your answers properly

IX. AFTER THE TEST

Scoring procedures differ in detail among civil service jurisdictions although the general principles are the same. Whether the papers are hand-scored or graded by machine we have described, they are nearly always graded by number. That is, the person who marks the paper knows only the number – never the name – of the applicant. Not until all the papers have been graded will they be matched with names. If other tests, such as training and experience or oral interview ratings have been given, scores will be combined. Different parts of the examination usually have different weights. For example, the written test might count 60 percent of the final grade, and a rating of training and experience 40 percent. In many jurisdictions, veterans will have a certain number of points added to their grades.

After the final grade has been determined, the names are placed in grade order and an eligible list is established. There are various methods for resolving ties between those who get the same final grade – probably the most common is to place first the name of the person whose application was received first. Job offers are made from the eligible list in the order the names appear on it. You will be notified of your grade and your rank as soon as all these computations have been made. This will be done as rapidly as possible.

People who are found to meet the requirements in the announcement are called "eligibles." Their names are put on a list of eligible candidates. An eligible's chances of getting a job depend on how high he stands on this list and how fast agencies are filling jobs from the list.

When a job is to be filled from a list of eligibles, the agency asks for the names of people on the list of eligibles for that job. When the civil service commission receives this request, it sends to the agency the names of the three people highest on this list. Or, if the job to be filled has specialized requirements, the office sends the agency the names of the top three persons who meet these requirements from the general list.

The appointing officer makes a choice from among the three people whose names were sent to him. If the selected person accepts the appointment, the names of the others are put back on the list to be considered for future openings.

That is the rule in hiring from all kinds of eligible lists, whether they are for typist, carpenter, chemist, or something else. For every vacancy, the appointing officer has his choice of any one of the top three eligibles on the list. This explains why the person whose name is on top of the list sometimes does not get an appointment when some of the persons lower on the list do. If the appointing officer chooses the second or third eligible, the No. 1 eligible does not get a job at once, but stays on the list until he is appointed or the list is terminated.

X. HOW TO PASS THE INTERVIEW TEST

The examination for which you applied requires an oral interview test. You have already taken the written test and you are now being called for the interview test – the final part of the formal examination.

You may think that it is not possible to prepare for an interview test and that there are no procedures to follow during an interview. Our purpose is to point out some things you can do in advance that will help you and some good rules to follow and pitfalls to avoid while you are being interviewed.

What is an interview supposed to test?

The written examination is designed to test the technical knowledge and competence of the candidate; the oral is designed to evaluate intangible qualities, not readily measured otherwise, and to establish a list showing the relative fitness of each candidate – as measured against his competitors – for the position sought. Scoring is not on the basis of "right" and "wrong," but on a sliding scale of values ranging from "not passable" to "outstanding." As a matter of fact, it is possible to achieve a relatively low score without a single "incorrect" answer because of evident weakness in the qualities being measured.

Occasionally, an examination may consist entirely of an oral test – either an individual or a group oral. In such cases, information is sought concerning the technical knowledges and abilities of the candidate, since there has been no written examination for this purpose. More commonly, however, an oral test is used to supplement a written examination.

Who conducts interviews?

The composition of oral boards varies among different jurisdictions. In nearly all, a representative of the personnel department serves as chairman. One of the members of the board may be a representative of the department in which the candidate would work. In some cases, "outside experts" are used, and, frequently, a businessman or some other representative of the general public is asked to serve. Labor and management or other special groups may be represented. The aim is to secure the services of experts in the appropriate field.

However the board is composed, it is a good idea (and not at all improper or unethical) to ascertain in advance of the interview who the members are and what groups they represent. When you are introduced to them, you will have some idea of their backgrounds and interests, and at least you will not stutter and stammer over their names.

What should be done before the interview?

While knowledge about the board members is useful and takes some of the surprise element out of the interview, there is other preparation which is more substantive. It *is* possible to prepare for an oral interview – in several ways:

1) Keep a copy of your application and review it carefully before the interview

This may be the only document before the oral board, and the starting point of the interview. Know what education and experience you have listed there, and the sequence and dates of all of it. Sometimes the board will ask you to review the highlights of your experience for them; you should not have to hem and haw doing it.

2) Study the class specification and the examination announcement

Usually, the oral board has one or both of these to guide them. The qualities, characteristics or knowledges required by the position sought are stated in these documents. They offer valuable clues as to the nature of the oral interview. For example, if the job involves supervisory responsibilities, the announcement will usually indicate that knowledge of modern supervisory methods and the qualifications of the candidate as a supervisor will be tested. If so, you can expect such questions, frequently in the form of a hypothetical situation which you are expected to solve. NEVER go into an oral without knowledge of the duties and responsibilities of the job you seek.

3) Think through each qualification required

Try to visualize the kind of questions you would ask if you were a board member. How well could you answer them? Try especially to appraise your own knowledge and background in each area, *measured against the job sought*, and identify any areas in which you are weak. Be critical and realistic – do not flatter yourself.

4) Do some general reading in areas in which you feel you may be weak

For example, if the job involves supervision and your past experience has NOT, some general reading in supervisory methods and practices, particularly in the field of human relations, might be useful. Do NOT study agency procedures or detailed manuals. The oral board will be testing your understanding and capacity, not your memory.

5) Get a good night's sleep and watch your general health and mental attitude

You will want a clear head at the interview. Take care of a cold or any other minor ailment, and of course, no hangovers.

What should be done on the day of the interview?

Now comes the day of the interview itself. Give yourself plenty of time to get there. Plan to arrive somewhat ahead of the scheduled time, particularly if your appointment is in the fore part of the day. If a previous candidate fails to appear, the board might be ready for you a bit early. By early afternoon an oral board is almost invariably behind schedule if there are many candidates, and you may have to wait. Take along a book or magazine to read, or your application to review, but leave any extraneous material in the waiting room when you go in for your interview. In any event, relax and compose yourself.

The matter of dress is important. The board is forming impressions about you – from your experience, your manners, your attitude, and your appearance. Give your personal appearance careful attention. Dress your best, but not your flashiest. Choose conservative, appropriate clothing, and be sure it is immaculate. This is a business interview, and your appearance should indicate that you regard it as such. Besides, being well groomed and properly dressed will help boost your confidence.

Sooner or later, someone will call your name and escort you into the interview room. *This is it.* From here on you are on your own. It is too late for any more preparation. But remember, you asked for this opportunity to prove your fitness, and you are here because your request was granted.

What happens when you go in?

The usual sequence of events will be as follows: The clerk (who is often the board stenographer) will introduce you to the chairman of the oral board, who will introduce you to the other members of the board. Acknowledge the introductions before you sit down. Do not be surprised if you find a microphone facing you or a stenotypist sitting by. Oral interviews are usually recorded in the event of an appeal or other review.

Usually the chairman of the board will open the interview by reviewing the highlights of your education and work experience from your application – primarily for the benefit of the other members of the board, as well as to get the material into the record. Do not interrupt or comment unless there is an error or significant misinterpretation; if that is the case, do not hesitate. But do not quibble about insignificant matters. Also, he will usually ask you some question about your education, experience or your present job – partly to get you to start talking and to establish the interviewing "rapport." He may start the actual questioning, or turn it over to one of the other members. Frequently, each member undertakes the questioning on a particular area, one in which he is perhaps most competent, so you can expect each member to participate in the examination. Because time is limited, you may also expect some rather abrupt switches in the direction the questioning takes, so do not be upset by it. Normally, a board member will not pursue a single line of questioning unless he discovers a particular strength or weakness.

After each member has participated, the chairman will usually ask whether any member has any further questions, then will ask you if you have anything you wish to add. Unless you are expecting this question, it may floor you. Worse, it may start you off on an extended, extemporaneous speech. The board is not usually seeking more information. The question is principally to offer you a last opportunity to present further qualifications or to indicate that you have nothing to add. So, if you feel that a significant qualification or characteristic has been overlooked, it is proper to point it out in a sentence or so. Do not compliment the board on the thoroughness of their examination -- they have been sketchy, and you know it. If you wish, merely say, "No thank you, I have nothing further to add." This is a point where you can "talk yourself out" of a good impression or fail to present an important bit of information. Remember, *you close the interview yourself.*

The chairman will then say, "That is all, Mr. _____, thank you." Do not be startled; the interview is over, and quicker than you think. Thank him, gather your belongings and take your leave. Save your sigh of relief for the other side of the door.

How to put your best foot forward

Throughout this entire process, you may feel that the board individually and collectively is trying to pierce your defenses, seek out your hidden weaknesses and embarrass and confuse you. Actually, this is not true. They are obliged to make an appraisal of your qualifications for the job you are seeking, and they want to see you in your best light. Remember, they must interview all candidates and a non-cooperative candidate may become a failure in spite of their best efforts to bring out his qualifications. Here are 15 suggestions that will help you:

1) Be natural – Keep your attitude confident, not cocky

If you are not confident that you can do the job, do not expect the board to be. Do not apologize for your weaknesses, try to bring out your strong points. The board is interested in a positive, not negative, presentation. Cockiness will antagonize any board member and make him wonder if you are covering up a weakness by a false show of strength.

2) Get comfortable, but don't lounge or sprawl

Sit erectly but not stiffly. A careless posture may lead the board to conclude that you are careless in other things, or at least that you are not impressed by the importance of the occasion. Either conclusion is natural, even if incorrect. Do not fuss with your clothing, a pencil or an ashtray. Your hands may occasionally be useful to emphasize a point; do not let them become a point of distraction.

3) Do not wisecrack or make small talk

This is a serious situation, and your attitude should show that you consider it as such. Further, the time of the board is limited – they do not want to waste it, and neither should you.

4) Do not exaggerate your experience or abilities
In the first place, from information in the application or other interviews and sources, the board may know more about you than you think. Secondly, you probably will not get away with it. An experienced board is rather adept at spotting such a situation, so do not take the chance.

5) If you know a board member, do not make a point of it, yet do not hide it
Certainly you are not fooling him, and probably not the other members of the board. Do not try to take advantage of your acquaintanceship – it will probably do you little good.

6) Do not dominate the interview
Let the board do that. They will give you the clues – do not assume that you have to do all the talking. Realize that the board has a number of questions to ask you, and do not try to take up all the interview time by showing off your extensive knowledge of the answer to the first one.

7) Be attentive
You only have 20 minutes or so, and you should keep your attention at its sharpest throughout. When a member is addressing a problem or question to you, give him your undivided attention. Address your reply principally to him, but do not exclude the other board members.

8) Do not interrupt
A board member may be stating a problem for you to analyze. He will ask you a question when the time comes. Let him state the problem, and wait for the question.

9) Make sure you understand the question
Do not try to answer until you are sure what the question is. If it is not clear, restate it in your own words or ask the board member to clarify it for you. However, do not haggle about minor elements.

10) Reply promptly but not hastily
A common entry on oral board rating sheets is "candidate responded readily," or "candidate hesitated in replies." Respond as promptly and quickly as you can, but do not jump to a hasty, ill-considered answer.

11) Do not be peremptory in your answers
A brief answer is proper – but do not fire your answer back. That is a losing game from your point of view. The board member can probably ask questions much faster than you can answer them.

12) Do not try to create the answer you think the board member wants
He is interested in what kind of mind you have and how it works – not in playing games. Furthermore, he can usually spot this practice and will actually grade you down on it.

13) Do not switch sides in your reply merely to agree with a board member
Frequently, a member will take a contrary position merely to draw you out and to see if you are willing and able to defend your point of view. Do not start a debate, yet do not surrender a good position. If a position is worth taking, it is worth defending.

14) Do not be afraid to admit an error in judgment if you are shown to be wrong

The board knows that you are forced to reply without any opportunity for careful consideration. Your answer may be demonstrably wrong. If so, admit it and get on with the interview.

15) Do not dwell at length on your present job

The opening question may relate to your present assignment. Answer the question but do not go into an extended discussion. You are being examined for a *new* job, not your present one. As a matter of fact, try to phrase ALL your answers in terms of the job for which you are being examined.

Basis of Rating

Probably you will forget most of these "do's" and "don'ts" when you walk into the oral interview room. Even remembering them all will not ensure you a passing grade. Perhaps you did not have the qualifications in the first place. But remembering them will help you to put your best foot forward, without treading on the toes of the board members.

Rumor and popular opinion to the contrary notwithstanding, an oral board wants you to make the best appearance possible. They know you are under pressure – but they also want to see how you respond to it as a guide to what your reaction would be under the pressures of the job you seek. They will be influenced by the degree of poise you display, the personal traits you show and the manner in which you respond.

ABOUT THIS BOOK

This book contains tests divided into Examination Sections. Go through each test, answering every question in the margin. We have also attached a sample answer sheet at the back of the book that can be removed and used. At the end of each test look at the answer key and check your answers. On the ones you got wrong, look at the right answer choice and learn. Do not fill in the answers first. Do not memorize the questions and answers, but understand the answer and principles involved. On your test, the questions will likely be different from the samples. Questions are changed and new ones added. If you understand these past questions you should have success with any changes that arise. Tests may consist of several types of questions. We have additional books on each subject should more study be advisable or necessary for you. Finally, the more you study, the better prepared you will be. This book is intended to be the last thing you study before you walk into the examination room. Prior study of relevant texts is also recommended. NLC publishes some of these in our Fundamental Series. Knowledge and good sense are important factors in passing your exam. Good luck also helps. So now study this Passbook, absorb the material contained within and take that knowledge into the examination. Then do your best to pass that exam.

EXAMINATION SECTION

EXAMINATION SECTION

TEST 1

DIRECTIONS: Each question or incomplete statement is followed by several suggested answers or completions. Select the one that BEST answers the question or completes the statement. *PRINT THE LETTER OF THE CORRECT ANSWER IN THE SPACE AT THE RIGHT.*

1. The owner's equity in a business may derive from which of the following sources?
   I. Excess of revenue over expenses
   II. Investment by the owner
   III. Accounts payable

   A. I only
   B. II only
   C. III only
   D. I and II
   E. I, II and III

   1._____

2. Entries made on the books at the end of a period to take care of changes occurring in accounts are called _____ entries.
   A. fiscal
   B. closing
   C. reversing
   D. correcting
   E. adjusting

   2._____

3. In accounting, net income should be defined as an increase in
   A. assets
   B. cash
   C. merchandise
   D. sales
   E. capital

   3._____

4. Treasury stock is CORRECTLY defined as
   A. a corporation's own stock that has been issued and then reacquired
   B. new issues of a corporation's stock before they are sold on the open market
   C. stock issued by the United States Office of the Treasury
   D. any stock that a corporation acquires and holds for more than 90 days
   E. any stock held by a corporation that receives dividends in excess of 5 percent of initial cost of the stock

   4._____

1

5. The Accumulated Depreciation account should be shown in the financial statements as
   A. an operating expense
   B. an extraordinary loss
   C. a liability
   D. stockholders' equity
   E. a contra (deduction) to an asset account

6. If fixed expenses are $26,000 and variable expenses are 75 percent of sales, the net income that would result from $500,000 in sales is
   A. $75,000
   B. $99,000
   C. $200,000
   D. $375,000
   E. $401,000

7. Cost of goods sold is determined by which of the following?
   A. Beginning inventory plus net purchases minus ending inventory
   B. Beginning inventory plus purchases plus purchase returns minus ending inventory
   C. Beginning inventory minus net purchases plus ending inventory
   D. Purchases minus transportation-in plus beginning inventory minus ending inventory
   E. Net sales minus ending inventory

8. Company X produces chairs of a single type, it has a plant capacity of 50,000 chairs per year and total fixed expenses of $100,000 per year. Variable costs per chair are $2.00 and the current selling price is $5.00 per chair. At the beginning of 2016, the company purchases a specialized machine that costs $10,000, lasts one year, and reduces variable costs to $1.50 per chair. If the company produces and sells at 90 percent of capacity, what is the net income for 2016?
   A. $8,750
   B. $23,000
   C. $47,500
   D. $50,000
   E. $83,000

9. All of the following T-accounts contain the correct sides that would be used for increasing and decreasing an account EXCEPT

   A. Revenue
       Decrease | Increase

   B. Assets
       Increase | Decrease

   C. Expenses
       Increase | Decrease

   D. Owner's Equity
       Increase | Decrease

   E. Liabilities
       Decrease | Increase

10. Green Corporation with assets of $5,000,000 and liabilities of $2,000,000 has 6,000 shares of capital stock outstanding (par value $300). What is the book value per share?
    A. $200
    B. $300
    C. $500
    D. $833
    E. None of the above

    10._____

11. Of the following, the BEST description of a controlling account is that it is a
    A. schedule of accounts payable
    B. purchase form that itemizes merchandise bought
    C. ledger that contains a single type of account
    D. statement that lists the individual account balances in the creditors' ledger
    E. general ledger account that summarizes the balance in the accounts of a subsidiary ledger

    11._____

12. At the end of the fiscal year, a company estimates that $4,300 of Accounts Receivable will be uncollectible. If, prior to adjustment, the company's Allowance for Bad Debts account has a credit balance of $1,600, what is the APPROPRIATE adjusting entry?

	Debit	Credit	Amount
A.	Allowance for Bad Debts	Bad Debts Expense	$4,300
B.	Allowance for Bad Debts	Accounts Receivable	$4,300
C.	Accounts Receivable	Allowance for Bad Debts	$1,600
D.	Bad Debts Expense	Allowance for Bad Debts	$2,700
E.	Bad Debts Expense	Accounts Receivable	$2,700

    12._____

13. A fast-moving widget stamping machine was purchased for cash. The list price was $4,000 with an applicable trade discount of 20 percent and a cash discount allowable of 2/10, n/30. Payment was made within the discount period. Freight costs of $100, F.O.B. origin, were paid. In order to install the machine properly, a platform was built and wiring installed for a total cost of $200. The trial run costs were $300 for labor and $50 for materials. The cost of the machine would be recorded as
    A. $3,626
    B. $3,628
    C. $3,786
    D. $3,828
    E. $4,178

    13._____

14. All of the following expenditures should be charged to an asset account rather than an expense account of the current period EXCEPT the cost of
    A. overhauling a delivery truck, which extends its useful life by two years
    B. purchasing a new component for a machine, which serves to increase the machine's productive capacity
    C. constructing a parking lot for a leased building
    D. installing a new piece of equipment
    E. replacing worn-out tires on a delivery truck

    14._____

15. In a period of rising prices, which of the following inventory methods results in the HIGHEST cost of goods sold?
    A. FIFO
    B. LIFO
    C. Average cost
    D. Periodic inventory
    E. Perpetual inventory

16. A company forecasts that during the next year it will be able to sell 80,000 units of its special product at a competitive selling price of $10 per unit. The company has the capacity to produce 120,000 units per year. Its total fixed costs are $528,000. Its variable costs are estimated at $3 per unit. The company has the opportunity to sell 10,000 additional units during the same year at a special contract price of $50,000. This special contract will not affect the regular sales volume or price.
    Acceptance of the contract will cause the year's net income to
    A. increase by $20,000
    B. increase by $26,000
    C. increase by $50,000
    D. decrease by $50,000
    E. decrease by $24,000

17. Which of the following standard cost variances provides information about the extent to which the manufacturing plant of a company was used at normal capacity?
    A. Materials quantity (usage) variance
    B. Labor efficiency (time) variance
    C. Labor rate variance
    D. Overhead spending (controllable) variance
    E. Overhead volume variance

18. The following information refers to the purchase of merchandise by L Company. List price of merchandise, $1,050; trade discount 20 percent, 2/10, n/30; F.O.B. shipping point; freight cost prepaid by seller and added to the invoice, $100. What is the net amount to be paid to the vendor, within the discount period, for the merchandise?
    A. $819.00
    B. $901.60
    C. $919.00
    D. $921.20
    E. $923.20

19. X Corporation declares and issues a 5 percent stock dividend on common stock, payable in common stock, shortly after the close of the year. All of the following statements about the nature and effect of the dividend are true EXCEPT:
    A. total stockholders' equity in the corporation is not changed
    B. dividend does not constitute income to the stockholders
    C. book value per share of common stock is not changed
    D. amount of retained earnings is reduced
    E. amount of total assets is not changed

20. The financial statement prepared to report the financing and investing activities of a business entity for a period of time is called the
    A. Income Statement
    B. Statement of Retained Earnings
    C. Balance Sheet
    D. Statement of Changes in Owners' Equity
    E. Statement of Changed in Financial Position

20._____

21. A feature of the process cost system that is NOT a feature of the job order cost system is
    A. computation of the equivalent units of production
    B. compilation of the costs of each batch or job produced
    C. use of the Raw Materials Inventory account
    D. preparation of a Cost of Goods Manufactured statement for each accounting period
    E. application of manufacturing overhead on a predetermined basis

21._____

22. Net purchases for the year amounted to $80,000. The merchandise inventory at the beginning of the year was $19,000. On sales of $120,000, a 30 percent gross profit on the selling price was realized. The inventory at the end of the year was
    A. $13,000
    B. $15,000
    C. $17,000
    D. $25,000
    E. $63,000

22._____

23. The balance sheet of Harold Company shows current assets of $200,000 and current liabilities of $100,000. The company uses cash to acquire merchandise inventory. As a result of this transaction, which of the following is TRUE of working capital and the current ratio?
    A. Both are unchanged
    B. Working capital is unchanged; the current ratio increases
    C. Both decrease
    D. Working capital decreases; the current ratio increases
    E. Working capital decreases; the current ratio is unchanged

23._____

24. *In determining net income from business operations, the costs involved in generating revenue should be charged against that revenue.*
    The statement above BEST describes the _____ principle.
    A. cost
    B. going-concern
    C. profit
    D. matching
    E. business entity

24._____

25. Which of the following is the BEST explanation of the amount reported on the balance sheet as accumulated depreciation?
    A. Self-insurance fund to protect against losses of the related assets from fire or other casualty
    B. Decrease in market value of the related assets
    C. Cash accumulated to purchase replacements as the related assets wear out
    D. Cost of the related assets which has been allocated to operations
    E. Estimated amount needed to replace the related assets as they wear out

25.____

KEY (CORRECT ANSWERS)

1. D	11. E	21. A
2. E	12. D	22. B
3. E	13. C	23. A
4. A	14. E	24. D
5. E	15. B	25. D
6. B	16. A	
7. A	17. E	
8. C	18. E	
9. D	19. C	
10. C	20. E	

TEST 2

DIRECTIONS: Each question or incomplete statement is followed by several suggested answers or completions. Select the one that BEST answers the question or completes the statement. *PRINT THE LETTER OF THE CORRECT ANSWER IN THE SPACE AT THE RIGHT.*

1. What is the number of days' inventory on hand for a firm with cost of goods sold of $750,000 and average ending inventory of $150,000?
   A. 5
   B. 10
   C. 20
   D. 50
   E. 73

   1._____

2. During the current year, accounts receivable increased from $27,000 to $41,000, and sales were $225,000. Based on this information, how much cash did the company collect from its customers during the year?
   A. $211,000
   B. $225,000
   C. $239,000
   D. $252,000
   E. $266,000

   2._____

3. Accounts receivable turnover helps determine
   A. the balance of accounts payable
   B. customers who have recently paid their bills
   C. how quickly a firm collects cash on its credit sales
   D. when to write off delinquent accounts
   E. credit sales

   3._____

4. The income statement is designed to measure
   A. whether a firm is able to pay its bills
   B. how solvent a company has been
   C. how much cash flow a firm is likely to generate
   D. the financial position of a firm
   E. the results of business operations

   4._____

5. A company prepares a bank reconciliation in order to
   A. determine the correct amount of the cash balance
   B. satisfy banking regulations
   C. determine deposits not yet recorded by the bank
   D. double-check the amount of petty cash
   E. record all check disbursements

   5._____

6. An inventory valuation method usually affects
   A. the cost of goods sold but not the balance sheet
   B. the balance sheet but not the cost of goods sold
   C. both the income statement and the balance sheet
   D. neither the income statement nor the balance sheet
   E. the cost of goods sold, but not the income statement

   6._____

7. A liability for dividends is recorded on the _____ date.
    A. declaration
    B. record
    C. payment
    D. collection
    E. statement

8. Assets are classified as intangible under which of the following conditions?
    A. They are converted into cash within one year
    B. They have no physical substance
    C. They are acquired in a merger
    D. They are long term and used in operations
    E. They are short term and used in operations

9. Return on assets helps users of financial statements evaluate which of the following?
    A. Profitability
    B. Liquidity
    C. Solvency
    D. Cash flow
    E. Reliability

10. The accounting concept that emphasizes the existence of a business firm separate and apart from its owners is ordinarily termed the ____ concept.
    A. business separation
    B. consistency
    C. going-concern
    D. business materiality
    E. business entity

11. Equity investors are most interested in which aspect(s) of a company?
    I. Book value
    II. Profitability
    III. Cash flow

    A. I only
    B. II only
    C. III only
    D. I and II only
    E. II and III only

12. One disadvantage of the corporation as compared to other types of business organizations is that
    A. greater legal liability is assigned to stockholders
    B. greater ethical responsibility is expected of officers and employees
    C. greater profit is required by owners
    D. shares of stock can be sold and transferred to new owners
    E. greater tax burden is levied on the entity

13. Land held for future use and not intended for operations should be classified as
    A. property, plant and equipment
    B. an intangible asset
    C. inventory
    D. an investment
    E. a current asset

14. If an individual borrows $95,000 on July 1 from Community Bank by signing a $95,000, 9 percent, one-year note, what is the accrued interest as of December 31?
    A. $0
    B. $2,138
    C. $4,275
    D. $6,413
    E. $8,550

15. In the preparation of the Statement of Cash Flows, which of the following transactions will NOT be reported as a financing activity?
    A. Sale of common stock
    B. Sale of bonds
    C. Issuance of long-term note to bank
    D. Issuance of 30-day note to trade creditor
    E. Purchase of treasury stock

16. A company bought a patent at a cost of $180,000. The patent had an original legal life of 17 years. The remaining legal life is 10 years, but the company expects its useful life will only be six years. When should the cost of the patent be charged to expenses?
    A. Immediately
    B. Over the next six years
    C. Over the next 10 years
    D. Over the next 17 years
    E. Over the next 40 years

17. How is treasury stock reported on the balance sheet?
    A. As an increase in liabilities
    B. As an increase in assets
    C. As a decrease in assets
    D. As an increase in stockholders' equity
    E. As a decrease in stockholders' equity

18. The selected accounts below are from TJ Supply's balance sheet. What is TJ Supply's working capital?

    Cash: $40,000
    Accounts receivable: $120,000
    Inventory: $300,000
    Prepaid rent: $2,000
    Accounts payable: $150,000
    Salaries payable: $7,000
    Long-term bonds payable: $200,000

    A. $40,000   B. $105,000
    C. $160,000   D. $305,000
    E. $462,000

19. A machine with a useful life of eight years was purchased for $600,000 on January 1. The estimated salvage value is $50,000.
    What is the first year's depreciation by using the double-declining-balance method?
    A. $50,000   B. $68,000
    C. $75,000   D. $137,500
    E. $150,000

20. Newman Corporation uses the allowance method of accounting for its accounts receivable. The company currently has a $100,000 balance in accounts receivable and a $5,000 balance in its allowance for uncollectible accounts. The company decides to write off $4,000 of its accounts receivable. What would be the balance in its net accounts receivable before and after the write-off?

	Before	After
A.	$95,000	$91,000
B.	$95,000	$95,000
C.	$100,000	$96,000
D.	$105,000	$101,000
E.	$105,000	$105,000

21. Trading securities must be reported on the balance sheet at
    A. historical cost
    B. cost plus earnings minus dividends
    C. book value
    D. fair market value
    E. net present value

22. An accrued expense results in
    A. an accrued liability
    B. an accrued revenue
    C. a prepaid expense
    D. an unearned revenue
    E. a contra owner's equity account

23. The L Company purchased new machinery and incurred the following costs:

Invoice price	$30,000
Freight (F.O.B. shipping point)	$2,000
Foundation for machinery	$1,000
Installation costs	$900
Annual maintenance of machinery	$600

    The total cost of the machinery is
    A. $30,000
    B. $31,900
    C. $32,000
    D. $33,900
    E. $34,500

24. Which of the following is true of annual depreciation expense?
    A. It represents the amount required for annual maintenance of a long-term asset
    B. It represents the annual revenue earned by an asset
    C. It allocates the cost of use of a long-term asset to the revenue that it generates
    D. It is required to fulfill the economic entity assumption
    E. It reduces cash

25. The matching concept matches
    A. customers with businesses
    B. expenses with revenues
    C. assets with liabilities
    D. creditors with businesses
    E. debits with credits

KEY (CORRECT ANSWERS)

1. E	11. E	21. D
2. A	12. E	22. A
3. C	13. D	23. D
4. E	14. C	24. C
5. A	15. D	25. B
6. C	16. B	
7. A	17. E	
8. B	18. D	
9. A	19. E	
10. E	20. B	

EXAMINATION SECTION
TEST 1

DIRECTIONS: Each question or incomplete statement is followed by several suggested answers or completions. Select the one that BEST answers the question or completes the statement. *PRINT THE LETTER OF THE CORRECT ANSWER IN THE SPACE AT THE RIGHT.*

1. A long-term liability of a corporation is represented by

   A. stock certificates issued
   B. stock subscriptions received
   C. the balance of a sinking fund
   D. bonds issued

2. Which is an advantage of incorporating?

   A. Establishing good will
   B. Acquiring treasury stock
   C. Limiting the liability of the owners
   D. Avoiding governmental control

3. Undistributed profits of a corporation are shown in the _____ account.

   A. earned surplus   B. treasury stock
   C. capital stock   D. bonds payable

4. The TOTAL amount of equity, or ownership, in a corporation is found by adding

   A. treasury stock and surplus
   B. capital stock and subscriptions
   C. capital stock and surplus
   D. capital stock and good will

5. On January 1, 2018, the earned surplus account of the Kalfur Corporation had a credit balance of $42,300. The net income for 2018 (after taxes) was $12,500. The dividends declared for 2018 amounted to $8,400.
   The balance of the earned surplus account on December 31, 2018 after the books were closed was

   A. $4,100   B. $33,900   C. $38,200   D. $46,400

6. The State Disability Benefits Insurance law provides benefits for an employee or his family when the employee

   A. dies
   B. retires
   C. is temporarily unable to work because of an off-the-job accident
   D. is temporarily unable to work because of an on-the-job accident

7. Which account does NOT belong in the current liability section of a balance sheet? _____ payable.

   A. Interest   B. Notes   C. Accounts   D. Mortgage

8. If the merchandise inventory on hand at the end of 2018 was overstated, what would be the effect?

   A. Understatement of income for 2018
   B. Overstatement of income for 2018
   C. Understatement of assets at the end of 2018
   D. No effect on income or assets

9. The face value of a 45-day, 6% promissory note is $740. The maturity value of the note will be

   A. $734.45   B. $740.00   C. $745.55   D. $747.40

10. When cash is received as a result of sales, the PROPER business procedure is to

    A. put the cash in the petty cash box
    B. deposit the cash in a checking account at the end of the day
    C. deposit the cash in a savings account at the end of the day
    D. use the cash to pay current bills

11. Which item can be determined from information on the Income Statement (Profit and Loss Statement)?

    A. Working capital
    B. Rate of merchandise turnover
    C. Total liabilities
    D. Owner's worth

12. Which item belongs on the Income Statement for the year?

    A. B. Rand, Drawing
    B. Accrued Salaries, Payable
    C. Purchases Discount
    D. Allowance for Depreciation of Furniture and Fixtures

13. _____ tax is affected by the number of exemptions claimed.

    A. FICA
    B. State unemployment insurance
    C. State income tax
    D. Federal unemployment insurance

14. The source of an entry in the Cash Payments Journal is a

    A. sales invoice   B. checkbook stub
    C. petty cash voucher   D. general ledger

15. If a partnership agreement does not indicate how profits and losses are to be divided, then they will be distributed

    A. equally
    B. in proportion to investment
    C. according to duties and responsibilities
    D. by a court

16. The two parties on a promissory note are known as the _____ and _____.

    A. drawee; maker
    B. drawee; drawer
    C. payee; drawee
    D. payee; maker

17. In order to find the correct available cash balance when reconciling the checkbook balance with the bank balance, outstanding checks should be _____ balance.

    A. added to the checkbook
    B. subtracted from the checkbook
    C. added to the bank
    D. subtracted from the bank

18. A check drawn by a bank on funds that it has on deposit in another bank is known as a

    A. bank draft
    B. certified check
    C. cashier's check
    D. money order

19. _____ tax is contributed by the employee and matched by the employer.

    A. State unemployment insurance
    B. State income tax
    C. FICA
    D. Federal unemployment insurance

20. Which general ledger account would appear in a post-closing trial balance?

    A. Interest Income
    B. Notes Receivable
    C. Sales Discount
    D. Bad Debts Expense

21. A time draft frequently used in connection with a purchase of merchandise is a

    A. trade acceptance
    B. check
    C. cashier's check
    D. bank draft

22. A list of accounts and their balances prepared from a subsidiary ledger is called a

    A. statement of account
    B. trial balance
    C. balance sheet
    D. schedule

23. A time draft which states on its face that it resulted from the sale or purchase of merchandise is called a

    A. promissory note
    B. purchase order
    C. bank draft
    D. trade acceptance

24. A truck is purchased for $14,800. It is estimated that the truck will be used for four years. At the end of the four years, it is estimated that the truck will have a scrap value of $10,900.
    The amount of annual depreciation is

    A. $3,900   B. $1,425   C. $1,200   D. $975

25. The current ratio is found by

    A. *dividing* current assets by current liabilities
    B. *subtracting* current liabilities from current assets
    C. *subtracting* total liabilities from total assets
    D. *dividing* current assets by net income

KEY (CORRECT ANSWERS)

1. D
2. C
3. A
4. C
5. D

6. C
7. D
8. B
9. C
10. B

11. B
12. C
13. C
14. B
15. A

16. D
17. D
18. A
19. C
20. B

21. A
22. D
23. D
24. D
25. A

TEST 2

DIRECTIONS: Each question or incomplete statement is followed by several suggested answers or completions. Select the one that BEST answers the question or completes the statement. *PRINT THE LETTER OF THE CORRECT ANSWER IN THE SPACE AT THE RIGHT.*

1. The Federal individual income tax return must be filed by

   A. December 31　　　　　B. March 15
   C. April 15　　　　　　　D. June 30

   1.____

2. When a firm discounts its own note at a bank, the account to be credited is

   A. Cash
   B. Notes Payable
   C. Notes Receivable Discounted
   D. Accounts Payable

   2.____

3. Brooks and Carton are partners with an investment of $50,000 and $25,000, respectively.
   How much should be credited to Brooks as his share of a $60,000 profit if their agreement provides that the partners are to share profits and losses in proportion to their investments?

   A. $20,000　　　B. $30,000　　　C. $40,000　　　D. $50,000

   3.____

4. At the end of the month, the total of the Schedule of Accounts Payable should equal the

   A. total of the Purchases column in the Purchases Journal
   B. total of the Accounts Payable column in the Cash Payments Journal
   C. balance of the Accounts Payable account in the General Ledger
   D. balance of the Purchases account in the General Ledger

   4.____

5. When depreciation on a fixed asset is recorded, the effect of the entry on the fundamental bookkeeping equation is that the

   A. assets and capital remain unchanged
   B. assets increase; capital decreases
   C. assets decrease; capital decreases
   D. assets decrease; capital increases

   5.____

6. The ORIGINAL source of an entry in the Purchases Journal is a

   A. purchase invoice　　　　B. stock inventory card
   C. purchase order　　　　　D. creditor's account

   6.____

7. The business form which is sent to each customer at the end of the month summarizing the transactions with him is called a

   A. schedule　　　　　　B. statement of account
   C. sales invoice　　　　D. voucher

   7.____

8. When we receive a bank draft from a customer, our bookkeeper should debit

   A. Notes Payable　　　　　B. Notes Receivable
   C. Accounts Receivable　　D. Cash

   8.____

9. The gross sales of a business are $170,000 and Sales Returns and Allowances $450. It is estimated that an additional allowance of 1% of net sales will be required. The amount listed for Bad Debts Expense on the Income Statement should be

   A. $1,250   B. $1,695.50   C. $1,700   D. $1,704.50

10. Which group of accounts will appear on a post-closing trial balance?

    A. Assets, liabilities, and expenses
    B. Income and expenses
    C. Liabilities, capital, and income
    D. Assets, liabilities, and capital

Questions 11-16.

DIRECTIONS: Questions 11 through 16 are to be answered SOLELY on the basis of the last part of the bank statement below, mailed to Arthur Greene for the month of June.

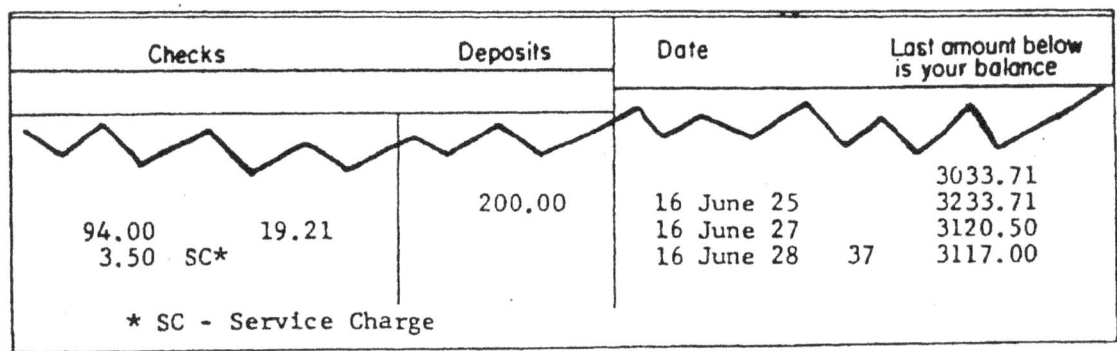

All the checks written have been paid except four. The last check written in June is No. 316. The stubs for the four outstanding checks are:

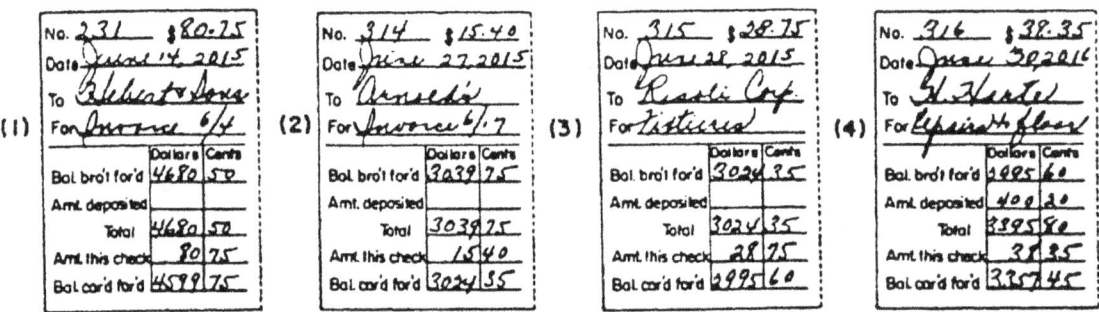

11. From the information available, what was Greene's corrected checkbook balance on June 30?

    A. $3,357.45   B. $3,117.00
    C. $3,353.95   D. $3,120.50

12. Which is the BEST reason that the deposit of $400.20, shown on Stub No. 316, does not appear on the bank statement?   12.____

    A. The bank has made an error.
    B. The bank has not credited his account.
    C. The withdrawals equal the deposits.
    D. The checks included in the deposit have not cleared the banks on which they were written.

13. When he examined the checks returned by his bank, Greene discovered that a check he had written for $44 had been incorrectly entered on the stub as $24.   13.____
    He should correct this error by

    A. adding $20 to his checkbook balance
    B. notifying his bank to add $20 to his account
    C. subtracting $20 from his checkbook balance
    D. subtracting $24 from his checkbook balance

14. On May 25, Greene wrote and had his bank certify a check for $150, which he mailed to Garcia, the payee. Garcia received the check on May 27 and deposited it in his bank on June 1. It was presented to Greene's bank and cleared for payment on June 2.   14.____
    On which date did Greene's bank deduct the $150 from his account?

    A. May 25   B. May 27   C. June 1   D. June 2

15. The journal entry to record the bank service charge shown on the bank statement should be made in the   15.____

    A. Petty Cashbook   B. General Journal
    C. Cash Receipts Journal   D. Cash Payments Journal

16. Greene's bookkeeper should prepare a bank reconciliation for June MAINLY to determine   16.____

    A. possible errors by comparing Greene's checkbook balance with the bank balance
    B. the total amount of checks written during the month
    C. which checks are still outstanding
    D. the total amount of cash deposited during the month

17. Which statement concerning a check is MOST accurate?   17.____

    A. A canceled check may be used to prove payment.
    B. Two signatures are required on each check drawn on a joint checking account.
    C. The corporation's name should be signed on the signature line of a check.
    D. Checks mailed for deposit should be endorsed by means of a blank endorsement.

18. If a check which has been certified is not used, which is the RECOMMENDED business practice?   18.____

    A. Mark the check *Void* and add the amount to the checkbook balance.
    B. Send a *stop payment* order to the bank.
    C. Deposit the check.
    D. Destroy the check.

19. Ames' bank returned a check which he had deposited, marked *N.S.F.* This notation indicates that the

   A. check has been improperly endorsed
   B. drawer has overdrawn his bank account
   C. drawer has stopped payment on the check
   D. signature on the check has been forged

20. In order to determine the correct available bank balance, the amount of a deposit made, but not yet recorded in an account, should be _____ balance.

   A. *added* to the checkbook
   B. *added* to the bank balance
   C. *subtracted* from the checkbook
   D. *subtracted* from the bank

Questions 21-25.

DIRECTIONS: Questions 21 through 25 are to be answered on the basis of the following depreciation record.

DEPRECIATION RECORD

Delivery Truck	Tractson	04387A	July 1, 2015
Asset	Make	Number	Acquired
$4,000	5 years	$500	straight-line
Cost	Estimated Life	Salvage Value	Meth. of Depr.

Year	1st quarter	2nd quarter	3rd quarter	4th quarter
1			$175	$175
2	...	...	$175	$175
3	$175	$175		
4	$175			
5				
6				

21. According to the record, the LAST adjusting entry had been made on or about

   A. June 1, 2015   B. June 1, 2016
   C. December 31, 2016   D. March 31, 2017

22. The book value on the date of the latest entry is

   A. $500   B. $2,275   C. $2,775   D. $3,500

23. The TOTAL amount of depreciation which would be recorded during the lifetime of the truck is

   A. $4,500   B. $4,000   C. $3,500   D. $500

24. What is the annual rate of depreciation for the truck?

   A. 17.5%   B. 2%   C. 20%   D. 5%

25. If a business uses the straight-line method of depreciation, which is CORRECT? 25._____
    A. All assets are depreciated at the same rate.
    B. The older the asset, the greater the amount of depreciation recorded each year.
    C. The rate of depreciation is the same each year for a particular asset.
    D. The salvage value will be the same for all fixed assets.

KEY (CORRECT ANSWERS)

1.	C	11.	C
2.	B	12.	B
3.	C	13.	C
4.	C	14.	A
5.	C	15.	D
6.	A	16.	A
7.	B	17.	A
8.	D	18.	C
9.	B	19.	B
10.	D	20.	B

21. D
22. C
23. C
24. A
25. C

TEST 3

DIRECTIONS: Each question or incomplete statement is followed by several suggested answers or completions. Select the one that BEST answers the question or completes the statement. *PRINT THE LETTER OF THE CORRECT ANSWER IN THE SPACE AT THE RIGHT.*

1. Entries in the Cash Payments Journal are USUALLY recorded from   1.____

    A. purchase invoices B. check stubs
    C. cancelled checks   D. expense sheets

2. A bank draft received from a customer is recorded in the   2.____

    A. General Journal   B. Note Register
    C. Sales Journal   D. Cash Receipts Journal

3. When sales taxes are collected from cash customers, the account credited is   3.____

    A. Sales Tax Payable   B. Sales Tax
    C. Cash   D. Accounts Payable

4. One advantage of the corporate form of business is   4.____

    A. limited life
    B. limited capital
    C. limited liability
    D. dissolution on death of an officer

5. Current assets minus current liabilities equals   5.____

    A. current turnover   B. current ratio
    C. asset ratio   D. working capital

6. What is the LATEST date that an invoice dated October 15 with terms net 10 E.O.M. should be paid?   6.____

    A. October 25   B. October 31
    C. November 10   D. November 30

7. The deduction allowed to a customer for an early payment of his account is known as a   7.____

    A. cash discount   B. mark down
    C. credit memorandum   D. trade discount

8. In a C.O.D. freight shipment, the business form that the seller attaches to the bill of lading is a   8.____

    A. sight draft   B. promissory note
    C. check   D. time draft

9. The form prepared to test the equality of debits and credits in the General Ledger is called   9.____

    A. statement of account   B. balance sheet
    C. trial balance   D. income statement

10. If the depreciation of a truck is calculated by the straight-line method, which statement is CORRECT?

    A. As the truck becomes older, the rate of depreciation increases.
    B. The rate of depreciation is the same each year.
    C. The amount of annual depreciation is based on the truck's mileage.
    D. On a statement of profit and loss, the depreciation appears as a deferred expense.

11. A computer program used to create spreadsheets, graphs and charts, and maintain financial records is

    A. Quickbooks
    B. Adobe Reader
    C. Microsoft Powerpoint
    D. Microsoft Excel

12. An inventory of merchandise prepared from an actual count of stock items on hand is described as a(n) _____ inventory.

    A. perpetual   B. physical   C. estimated   D. fixed

13. Which is NOT classified as a current asset on the balance sheet?

    A. Petty Cash
    B. Notes Receivable
    C. Land
    D. Accounts Receivable

14. Which error will cause a trial balance to be out of balance?

    A. Failure to post the debit part of a journal entry
    B. Failure to record an entire journal entry
    C. Error in totaling the sales journal
    D. Posting a debit in the debit side of the wrong account

15. If a customer's check which you had deposited is returned to you by the bank labeled *dishonored*, what entry would be made?
    Debit

    A. Cash and credit customer's account
    B. Miscellaneous Expense and credit Cash
    C. customer's account and credit Capital
    D. customer's account and credit Cash

16. The total of the Purchases Journal for the month of May was incorrectly computed as $6,500. The correct amount was $5,500. The $6,500 was used to record and post the summary entry for the month.
    To correct the error, the bookkeeper should debit

    A. Merchandise Purchases and credit Accounts Payable $5,500
    B. Merchandise Purchases and credit Accounts Payable $1,000
    C. Accounts Payable and credit Merchandise Purchases $1,000
    D. Accounts Payable and credit Merchandise Purchases $6,500

17. Entries in the Purchases Journal are USUALLY recorded from

    A. purchase requisitions
    B. purchase invoices
    C. check stubs
    D. credit memorandums

18. Merchandise was sold on April 10, 2018 for $400 less a trade discount of 25%, terms 2/10, n/30.
The amount required to settle the invoice on April 20 is

   A. $294   B. $300   C. $392   D. $400

19. When the books were closed at the end of the business fiscal year, there was a failure to record depreciation on Office Equipment for the year.
This error had the effect of

   A. *understating* the book value of the asset Office Equipment
   B. *overstating* the book value of the asset Office Equipment
   C. *understating* the net income of the asset Office Equipment
   D. *overstating* operating expenses

Questions 20-25.

DIRECTIONS: Questions 20 through 25 are to be answered SOLELY on the basis of the following bank reconciliation statement.

CONDON, INC. Bank Reconciliation March 31.			
Checkbook balance	$3,148.70	Bank Balance	$3,830.65
Less: Service Charge	4.15	Add: Deposit in Transit	310.00
		Total	4,140.65
		Less: Outstanding Checks	
		No. 815 $470.20	
		817 525.90	996.10
		(No. 813 certified 920.00)	
Adjusted checkbook balance	$3,144.55	Available bank balance	$3,144.55

20. Which entry will be made on the books of Condon, Inc. to record the bank service charge?
Debit

   A. Cash, credit Bank Charges
   B. Bank Charges, credit Accounts Payable
   C. Bank Charges, credit Cash
   D. Bank Account, credit Bank Charges

21. The deposit in transit of $310 will be listed on the

   A. bank statement for the month of March
   B. bank statement for the month of April
   C. bank statement for the month of February
   D. check stub record *only*

22. The bookkeeper determined which checks were outstanding by

    A. counting the cancelled checks
    B. examining the bank statement
    C. comparing the cancelled checks with the bank statement
    D. comparing the cancelled checks with the check stubs

23. The certified check of $920 was NOT deducted with the other outstanding checks because it

    A. was deducted from our bank balance at the time it was certified
    B. was not deducted from our checkbook balance when it was written
    C. will not be cashed by our bank
    D. will not be deducted from our bank balance until it clears our bank

24. The MAIN reason for preparing the bank reconciliation statement is to determine the

    A. total amount of cancelled checks
    B. total amount of outstanding checks
    C. total deposits with withdrawals for the month
    D. errors that might have been made

25. A trial balance is prepared to

    A. see if the totals agree with the subsidiary ledgers
    B. see if the total debit balances in the General Ledger agree with the total credit balances in the General Ledger
    C. show the worth of the business
    D. make up statements of customers' accounts

KEY (CORRECT ANSWERS)

1.	B	11.	D
2.	D	12.	B
3.	A	13.	C
4.	C	14.	A
5.	D	15.	D
6.	C	16.	C
7.	A	17.	B
8.	A	18.	A
9.	C	19.	B
10.	B	20.	C

21. B
22. D
23. A
24. D
25. B

TEST 4

DIRECTIONS: Each question or incomplete statement is followed by several suggested answers or completions. Select the one that BEST answers the question or completes the statement. *PRINT THE LETTER OF THE CORRECT ANSWER IN THE SPACE AT THE RIGHT.*

1. The due date of a 60-day promissory note dated June 15 is August

    A. 13 B. 14 C. 15 D. 16

2. Using the information that can be found in the Income Statement, one can find the

    A. current ratio
    B. merchandise turnover
    C. working capital
    D. rate of return on capital

3. Which of the following is NOT a computer program commonly used for accounting and finance purposes?

    A. QuarkXPress   B. Peachtree
    C. Quicken   D. Quickbooks

4. The ABC Corporation has 100,000 shares of stock outstanding. The Corporation decides to distribute to the stockholders a $200,000 profit.
If a stockholder owns 100 shares of stock, he will receive a TOTAL dividend of

    A. $50.00 B. $2.00 C. $200.00 D. $.50

5. A transaction that will cause a DECREASE in capital is a

    A. purchase of office equipment on credit
    B. payment of a creditor's account less a cash discount
    C. payment of an interest-bearing note
    D. prepayment of freight for a customer, to be charged to the customer's account

6. Mr. Davis is married and has three children who go to school. His oldest son, age 17, earned $900 during the year working parttime.
On his joint Federal income tax return, Mr. Davis may claim a MAXIMUM of _____ exemptions.

    A. five B. two C. three D. four

7. If the total of the Schedule of Accounts Receivable does not agree with the balance in the Accounts Receivable Controlling account, the difference may have been caused by

    A. adding the Sales Journal incorrectly
    B. failing to enter a sale in the Sales Journal
    C. posting a sale to the wrong customer's account
    D. failing to record a check received from a customer

8. An entry in the general journal is USUALLY made from the

    A. sales invoice   B. purchase invoice
    C. credit memorandum   D. incoming check

9. An example of a tax collected by the Federal government is the 9.____

   A. sales tax
   B. real estate tax
   C. automobile registration fee
   D. social security tax

10. The adjusting entry at the end of the year to record the estimated depreciation for the year results in a(n) 10.____

    A. *increase* in liabilities and a decrease in capital
    B. *decrease* in assets and an increase in assets
    C. *decrease* in assets and a decrease in capital
    D. *decrease* in assets and an increase in capital

11. On December 28, the total in the Salaries Expense Account was $59,500. On December 31, the bookkeeper recorded accrued salaries of $600. 11.____
    The entry to close the Salaries Expense Account on December 31 should be debit the _____ and credit the _____.

    A. Income and Expense Summary Account for $59,500; Salaries Expense Account for $59,500
    B. Income and Expense Summary Account for $60,100; Salaries Expense Account for $60,100
    C. Income and Expense Summary Account for $58,900; Salaries Expense Account for $58,900
    D. Salaries Expense Account for $59,500; Income and Expense Summary Account for $59,500

12. The tax paid by the employee to provide benefits upon his retirement is the 12.____

    A. FICA tax
    B. State Disability Benefits
    C. Federal withholding tax
    D. workmen's compensation insurance

13. The Federal income tax form that is given to the employee to show his total salary for the year and the amount of withholding tax for the year is called Form 13.____

    A. 941   B. W-4   C. 1099   D. W-2

14. An error that would cause the trial balance to be out of balance would be INCORRECTLY adding 14.____

    A. the Purchase Journal
    B. the cash column in the Cash Receipts Journal
    C. the Schedule of Accounts Receivable
    D. extensions on an invoice

15. An account that would be shown in a post-closing trial balance is 15.____

    A. Notes Receivable   B. Sales Income
    C. Discount on Purchases   D. Freight Out

16. You have just posted an entry from the Sales Journal to the customer's account. The correct amount in the Sales Journal is $125, but you posted $12.50.
To correct the error, you should

    A. draw a single line through the $12.50 in the account and write $125 above it
    B. debit in the General Journal the customer's account for $112.50 and credit the Sales Income Account for $112.50
    C. credit in the General Journal the customer's account for $12.50 and debit the Sales Income Account for $12.50
    D. debit in the Sales Journal the customer's account for $112.50 and credit the Sales Income Account for $112.50

17. When the bookkeeper added the trial balance, she found that it did not balance.
To find the reason, a logical FIRST step would be to

    A. check the pencil footings in ledger accounts
    B. add the trial balance a second time
    C. check whether figures were copied correctly from the ledger to the trial balance
    D. check postings from the journals

18. A column or group of columns containing data of a specific nature on a punched card is called a

    A. zone   B. field   C. row   D. file

19. *Allowance for Doubtful Accounts* is BEST described as a(n) _____ account.

    A. contingent liability   B. capital
    C. expense   D. asset valuation

20. A sales invoice to Judy Burns for $50 was entered in the Sales Journal as $150.
Which would occur as a result of this error?
The

    A. trial balance will not balance at the end of the month
    B. balance of the monthly statement to Judy Burns will be overstated
    C. check received from Judy Burns in payment of her account will be larger than the correct amount
    D. Accounts Receivable controlling account will not agree with the Schedule of Accounts Receivable at the end of the month

21. Sales taxes which are collected from customers and which will subsequently be remitted to the State Tax Bureau are recorded by the retailer as a(n)

    A. operating expense in the Income Statement
    B. addition to sales in the Income Statement
    C. current asset in the Balance Sheet
    D. current liability in the Balance Sheet

22. When the payee of a check writes as an endorsement *Pay to the order of (name of the firm)* before his signature, he has used a _____ endorsement.

    A. blank   B. qualified
    C. restrictive   D. full

23. Entries in the Purchases Journal are USUALLY made from which source document?   23.____

    A. Purchase order
    B. Purchase requisition
    C. Incoming invoice
    D. Outgoing invoice

24. Which is shown on the bank statement sent by the bank each month?   24.____

    A. Outstanding checks
    B. Deposits in transit
    C. Checks paid by the bank during the month
    D. The amount of interest earned during the month

25. The authorization by the State of New York which permits a group of persons to do business as a corporation is called the   25.____

    A. charter
    B. by-laws
    C. trade acceptance
    D. articles of copartnership

KEY (CORRECT ANSWERS)

1. B
2. B
3. A
4. C
5. C

6. A
7. A
8. C
9. D
10. C

11. B
12. A
13. D
14. B
15. A

16. A
17. B
18. B
19. D
20. B

21. D
22. D
23. C
24. C
25. A

EXAMINATION SECTION
TEST 1

DIRECTIONS: Each question or incomplete statement is followed by several suggested answers or completions. Select the one that BEST answers the question or completes the statement. *PRINT THE LETTER OF THE CORRECT ANSWER IN THE SPACE AT THE RIGHT.*

Questions 1-5.

DIRECTIONS: Questions 1 through 5 are to be answered on the basis of the following information.

The balance on our bank statement is $6,842.50. The bank had made a service charge of $4.50. Our check stubs reveal a final balance of $5,747.50. A comparison of the check stubs with the bank statement indicated that a deposit we had mailed on the 29th for $585 had not been recorded by the monthly closing. Four checks which we had made out ($1,001, $645, $38.50, and a certified check for $1,200) had not been cleared by the monthly closing.

1. The effect of the deposit in transit is to _____ balance.

    A. *increase* the final check stub
    B. *decrease* the final check stub
    C. *increase* the bank
    D. *decrease* the bank

2. The effect of the bank service charge is to _____ balance.

    A. *increase* the final check stub
    B. *decrease* the final check stub
    C. *increase* the bank
    D. *decrease* the bank

3. The CORRECTED check stub balance after reconciliation is

    A. $5,743   B. $5,752   C. $6,337   D. $6,843

4. The TOTAL of the outstanding checks to be subtracted from the bank balance is

    A. $484.50   B. $1,684.50   C. $2,269.50   D. $2,885.50

5. The CORRECTED bank balance after reconciliation is

    A. $5,743   B. $5,789   C. $6,843   D. $7,428

Questions 6-8.

DIRECTIONS: Questions 6 through 8 are to be answered on the basis of the worksheet below, which is for the first quarter of the Argo Taxi Company.

2 (#1)

[Worksheet image: ARGO TAXI CO., INC WORKSHEET FOR QUARTER ENDED 3/31/-- with columns for Trial Balance, Adjustments, Income Statement, Balance Sheet]

6. The balance of the Automobiles account after the June adjustment is 6._____

   A. $8,750   B. $23,000   C. $31,750   D. $105,000

7. The book value of the asset Maintenance Equipment, after adjusting entries, is 7._____

   A. $7,500   B. $12,500   C. $13,000   D. $20,000

8. Assuming that the entire net profit after taxes was transferred to Retained Earnings, the balance of the Retained Earnings account would be 8._____

   A. $10,252.50 B. $13,200
   C. $23,452.50 D. $36,652.50

9. The TOTAL operating expenses for the quarter were 9._____

   A. $13,530   B. $48,730   C. $121,450   D. $192,200

10. Closing entries are prepared from _____ columns. 10._____

    A. Trial Balance   B. Adjustment
    C. Income Statement   D. Balance Sheet

11. When sales taxes are collected from cash customers, the account credited is 11._____

    A. Sales Taxes Payable   B. Sales Taxes
    C. Cash   D. Accounts Payable

12. What type of data processing equipment would arrange punched cards alphabetically? 12._____

    A. Card punch   B. Card verifier
    C. Sorter   D. Tabulator

13. _____ tax is affected by the number of exemptions claimed by the employee. 13._____

    A. State Unemployment Insurance   B. Federal Unemployment Insurance
    C. FICA   D. Federal income

14. The merchandise turnover is found by dividing _____ merchandise inventory.   14.____

    A. net sales by ending
    B. net sales by average
    C. cost of goods sold by average
    D. cost of goods sold by ending

15. The process of summarizing the income and expense accounts and transferring the net   15.____
    result to the Retained Earnings account is known as

    A. adjusting the accounts
    B. reversing the accounts
    C. closing the ledger
    D. preparing a post-closing trial balance

16. An example of a fixed asset is   16.____

    A. equipment   B. merchandise inventory
    C. cash   D. prepaid insurance

17. Determining that the amount of cash on hand agrees with the balance of the cash   17.____
    account is known as

    A. recording
    B. proving cash
    C. reconciling the bank statement
    D. establishing the petty cash fund

18. The balance in the Accounts Receivable controlling account on December 31 is $20,500.   18.____
    The balance in the Allowance for Bad Debts account is $750 after adjustments.
    The amount believed to be collectible from customers is

    A. $750   B. $19,750   C. $20,500   D. $21,250

19. The FIRST record of any transaction of a business is made in the   19.____

    A. ledger   B. account
    C. journal   D. balance sheet

20. A decrease in owner's capital that results from a business transaction is called   20.____

    A. income   B. expense   C. asset   D. liability

21. The difference between the sales and the cost of goods sold is called   21.____

    A. net sales   B. sales returns
    C. gross profit on sales   D. sales discount

22. A customer sent a check for $50 in partial payment of her account.   22.____
    What would be the effect of erroneously posting the check as a debit to the customer's
    account?

    A. *Overstatement* of the total of the Schedule of Accounts Receivable
    B. *Understatement* of the Accounts Receivable controlling account
    C. *Overstatement* of the Accounts Receivable controlling account
    D. *Understatement* of the total of the Schedule of Accounts Receivable

23. In the absence of any statement in the partnership agreement as to the manner of sharing profits and losses, such profits and losses will be shared

    A. equally
    B. according to investments
    C. according to work performed
    D. according to sales

24. At the end of the year, which account should be closed into the Income and Expense Summary account?

    A. Petty Cash
    B. Depreciation of Furniture and Fixtures
    C. Allowance for Bad Debts
    D. Notes Payable

25. On an Income Statement, losses from bad debts will appear as a(n)

    A. operating expense
    B. deduction from Accounts Receivable
    C. addition to the cost of goods sold
    D. deduction from the cost of goods sold

KEY (CORRECT ANSWERS)

1. C	11. A
2. B	12. C
3. A	13. D
4. B	14. C
5. A	15. C
6. D	16. A
7. B	17. B
8. D	18. B
9. B	19. C
10. C	20. B

21. C
22. A
23. A
24. B
25. A

TEST 2

DIRECTIONS: Each question or incomplete statement is followed by several suggested answers or completions. Select the one that BEST answers the question or completes the statement. *PRINT THE LETTER OF THE CORRECT ANSWER IN THE SPACE AT THE RIGHT.*

1. A bookkeeping worksheet is prepared

    A. to be used as a source document
    B. to distribute to the stockholders at the end of the year
    C. as an aid in the preparation of financial statements
    D. to be used as a financial statement

2. When a set of books for a partnership is opened, the CORRECT procedure is to set up

    A. a capital account for each partner
    B. a capital account for each partner except *silent* partners
    C. one capital account that would show the combined investment of the partners
    D. an account showing stock already subscribed

3. At the end of the fiscal period, it is determined that the interest owed and not paid on the mortgage amounts to $420. This amount will be debited to

    A. Interest Expense
    B. Mortgage Payable
    C. Interest Receivable
    D. Interest Income

4. Income that has been earned but not yet received is referred to as _____ income.

    A. deferred   B. accrued   C. unearned   D. prepaid

5. The account Mortgage Payable is a(n)

    A. current liability
    B. prepaid expense
    C. accrued expense
    D. fixed liability

6. Under the cash basis of keeping books, all items of income are recorded when

    A. paid   B. billed   C. received   D. ordered

7. A financial statement prepared by a data processing system is an example of

    A. a source document
    B. output
    C. a flowchart
    D. input

8. On an income statement, net sales minus cost of goods sold is the

    A. gross profit
    B. merchandise available for sale
    C. net operating profit
    D. net profit before taxes

9. Allowance for Depreciation of Delivery Equipment is a(n) _____ account.

    A. liability   B. expense   C. accrual   D. valuation

10. When the totals of the two columns of a Trial Balance are equal, it proves that

    A. all debits and credits have been posted to the proper accounts
    B. there have been no offsetting errors
    C. no entries have been omitted
    D. equal amounts of debits and credits have been posted

11. The TOTAL of the Sales Journal is posted as a debit to

    A. Accounts Receivable   B. Accounts Payable
    C. Sales   D. Cash

12. Unexpired insurance is recorded as a debit to

    A. Insurance Receivable   B. Prepaid Insurance
    C. Insurance Payable   D. Insurance Expense

13. The cost price of a fixed asset minus the Allowance for Depreciation is known as its _____ value.

    A. cash   B. par   C. market   D. book

14. The payment in cash by The Lake Corporation on April 1, 2008 of a dividend declared and recorded on March 10, 2008 results in

    A. a decrease in assets and a decrease in capital
    B. both an increase and a decrease in assets
    C. a decrease in assets and a decrease in liabilities
    D. a decrease in liabilities and an increase in capital

15. Current assets minus current liabilities equals

    A. current ratio   B. current turnover
    C. merchandise turnover   D. working capital

16. The proprietor withdrew cash for his personal use. The effect on the fundamental book-keeping equation is to

    A. *increase* assets and decrease owner's worth
    B. *increase* assets and increase owner's worth
    C. *decrease* assets and decrease liabilities
    D. *decrease* assets and decrease owner's worth

17. A payment for gasoline and oil was incorrectly debited to the Delivery Equipment account instead of to the Delivery Expense account.
    This error, if not corrected, would result in

    A. understatement of the total assets
    B. no effect on the net profit
    C. an understatement of the net profit
    D. an overstatement of the net profit

18. A bookkeeper made an entry debiting the Bad Debts Expense account and crediting the Allowance for Bad Debts account. The credit represents a(n)

    A. *increase* in the liabilities
    B. *increase* in the net worth

C. *decrease* in the value of the assets
D. *decrease* in the liabilities

19. Adjusting entries are NORMALLY made

    A. before the Trial Balance is taken
    B. whenever price changes occur in inventory costs
    C. at the beginning of each fiscal period
    D. at the end of the current fiscal period

20. The declaration of a cash dividend by the Yule Corporation will result in a(n)

    A. *increase* in assets and an increase in liabilities
    B. *increase* in liabilities and a decrease in capital
    C. *decrease* in assets and a decrease in liabilities
    D. *decrease* in assets and a decrease in capital

21.

Accounts Payable

May	31		CP6	178	00	May	31				
	31		J4	80	00				P3	320	00
June	2		J5	75	00						

The above account was taken from the General Ledger of Clarke & Scott. The above account is classified as a

A. fixed liability   B. contingent asset
C. deferred asset   D. current liability

22. When a corporation declares a dividend on its stock, the account debited is

    A. Dividends Payable   B. Retained Earnings
    C. Capital Stock   D. Stock Subscriptions

23. The payroll tax for the State unemployment insurance is paid by

    A. the employee *only*
    B. both the employee and the employer
    C. the employer *only*
    D. the insurance company

24. Which computer application would MOST likely be used for accounting purposes?

    A. Microsoft Powerpoint   B. Adobe Reader
    C. Internet Explorer   D. Microsoft Excel

25. A diagram of a bookkeeping operation through a computerized system is called a

    A. floor plan   B. worksheet
    C. flowchart   D. CPU

KEY (CORRECT ANSWERS)

1.	C	11.	A
2.	A	12.	B
3.	A	13.	D
4.	B	14.	C
5.	D	15.	D
6.	C	16.	D
7.	B	17.	D
8.	A	18.	C
9.	D	19.	D
10.	D	20.	B

21. D
22. B
23. C
24. D
25. C

TEST 3

DIRECTIONS: Each question or incomplete statement is followed by several suggested answers or completions. Select the one that BEST answers the question or completes the statement. *PRINT THE LETTER OF THE CORRECT ANSWER IN THE SPACE AT THE RIGHT.*

1. The process of transferring information from the journal to the ledger is called

   A. journalizing
   B. posting
   C. closing
   D. balancing

2. Which is NOT an asset account?

   A. Supplies on Hand
   B. Prepaid Insurance
   C. Office Equipment
   D. Sales

3. Which journal entries are used at the end of each accounting period to clear the balances from the temporary accounts so that these accounts may be used in accumulating data for preparing the next period's statement. _____ entries.

   A. Correcting
   B. Closing
   C. Adjusting
   D. Opening

4. The verification of the equality of debits and credits in the General Ledger is called a

   A. trial balance
   B. schedule
   C. statement
   D. worksheet

5. Which account would NOT be listed on the Balance Sheet as a current liability?

   A. Accounts Payable
   B. Sales Taxes Payable
   C. Mortgage Payable
   D. FICA Taxes Payable

6. Debts owed by a business enterprise are referred to as

   A. capital   B. income   C. assets   D. liabilities

7. If insurance premiums were recorded as an asset when paid, the adjusting entry needed to record the expired insurance would require a debit to which account?

   A. Miscellaneous Expense
   B. Prepaid Insurance
   C. Insurance Expense
   D. John Green, Capital

8. A diagram showing the sequence of steps involved in an automated data processing procedure is called a

   A. flowchart
   B. source document
   C. coding sheet
   D. spreadsheet

9. If a business enterprise paid $3,000 to its creditors on account, what was the effect of the transaction on the accounting equation? A(n)

   A. *increase* in an asset, an increase in a liability
   B. *decrease* in an asset, a decrease in a liability
   C. *increase* in an asset, an increase in capital
   D. *increase* in one asset, a decrease in another asset

10. Which three steps of an automated data processing system are listed in the PROPER order?

    A. Input, storage, process
    B. Process, data origination, output
    C. Output, input, storage
    D. Input, process, output

11. The Merchandise Inventory account is GENERALLY adjusted

    A. when inventory is purchased
    B. when inventory is sold
    C. at the end of the accounting period
    D. at the beginning of each month

12. Which transaction is recorded in the Sales Journal? The sale of

    A. merchandise for cash
    B. merchandise on account
    C. vacant land (plant asset) for cash
    D. vacant land (plant asset) on account

13. Which is an example of a transposition error? Recording $450 as

    A. $540   B. $4,500.00   C. $455   D. $4.50

14. The accounting equation is CORRECTLY stated as

    A. Owner's Equity = Assets + Liabilities
    B. Owner's Equity - Assets = Liabilities
    C. Owner's Equity = Liabilities - Assets
    D. Assets = Liabilities + Owner's Equity

15. The Wage and Tax statement, Form W-2, is a form which shows

    A. a listing of deductions taken from an employee's salary
    B. an end-of-year listing of total wages and income tax and FICA withholdings
    C. the bonds purchased for an employee by an employer
    D. the marital status of an employee and the number of allowances claimed

16. A set of instructions which guides the processing of data by an electronic computer is called a

    A. file   B. diagram   C. program   D. record

17. An invoice is dated June 3. Terms of the sale are n/45. What is the LAST date for payment?   17.____

    A. June 30   B. July 17   C. July 18   D. July 19

18. The accounting equation is summarized in the   18.____

    A. Balance Sheet
    B. Trial Balance
    C. Income Statement
    D. Schedule of Accounts Payable

19. The Accounts Payable Subsidiary Ledger contains the amounts   19.____

    A. owed to the business by charge customers
    B. owed by the business to creditors
    C. of all cash purchases of merchandise
    D. of all sales discounts

20. Which procedure is followed in a journalless accounting system for handling accounts receivable?   20.____

    A. A trial balance must be prepared daily.
    B. Debits do not equal credits at the end of the accounting period when all postings have been made.
    C. Individual sales are recorded in a multicolumn Sales Journal instead of in a one-column Sales Journal.
    D. Posting to customers' accounts is made directly from the sales invoices.

21. _____ is a voluntary payroll deduction.   21.____

    A. FICA tax   B. Credit union savings
    C. Federal withholding tax   D. State income tax

22. On a worksheet, if the Trial Balance debit column is larger than the Trial Balance credit column, it indicates a(n)   22.____

    A. net income   B. net loss
    C. error   D. decrease in capital

23. In the General Ledger, the controlling account that summarizes the activities in the Customer's Ledger is called   23.____

    A. Accounts Receivable   B. Accounts Payable
    C. Purchases   D. Sales

24. The balance of the Insurance Expense account in the Income Statement debit column on the worksheet represents the   24.____

    A. insurance expired during the fiscal period
    B. face value of all insurance policies
    C. value of the prepaid insurance at the end of the fiscal period
    D. cash value of all insurance policies

25. A fee paid to the bank when securing a cashier's check should be recorded by a debit to   25.____
    _____ and a credit to _____.
    A. Petty Cash; Cash
    B. Miscellaneous Expense; Bank Charges
    C. Accounts Receivable; Cash
    D. Miscellaneous Expense; Cash

KEY (CORRECT ANSWERS)

1.	B	11.	C
2.	D	12.	B
3.	B	13.	A
4.	A	14.	D
5.	C	15.	B
6.	D	16.	C
7.	C	17.	C
8.	A	18.	A
9.	B	19.	B
10.	D	20.	D

21. B
22. C
23. A
24. A
25. D

TEST 4

DIRECTIONS: Each question or incomplete statement is followed by several suggested answers or completions. Select the one that BEST answers the question or completes the statement. *PRINT THE LETTER OF THE CORRECT ANSWER IN THE SPACE AT THE RIGHT.*

1. A 60-day promissory note dated April 12 will be due on June

   A. 11   B. 12   C. 13   D. 14

2. Failure to set up an allowance for doubtful accounts at the end of 2012 will result in an _____ 2012.

   A. *understatement* of net profit for
   B. *overstatement* of net profit for
   C. *understatement* of assets at the end of
   D. *overstatement* of liabilities at the end of

3. Which error will cause the trial balance to be out of balance?

   A. Forgetting to post from the Sales Journal to the H. Allen account in the Accounts Receivable Ledger
   B. Failing to record the purchase of a desk
   C. Incorrectly totaling the Purchase Journal
   D. Posting the $1,250 total of the accounts receivable column in the Cash Receipts Journal as $1,520

4. The checkbook balance on May 2, at the start of the day, was $1,500. During the day, a deposit of $75 was made, and checks for $100 and $50 were written. What was the checkbook balance at the end of the day?

   A. $1,275   B. $1,425   C. $1,575   D. $1,725

5. Data about Accounts Receivable to be fed into an automatic data processing system is often recorded in the form of

   A. statements of account
   B. punched cards
   C. schedule of accounts receivable
   D. sales journals

6. A purchase of merchandise on credit results in a(n) _____ in assets and a(n) _____ in liabilities.

   A. increase; increase   B. increase; decrease
   C. decrease; decrease   D. decrease; increase

7. During her vacation, Harriet Miller, age 45, was injured while driving her own car. For part of the 5 weeks she was unable to work, cash benefits MOST likely would be paid to her under

   A. Workers' Compensation
   B. the Social Security Administration

C. State Disability Benefits Insurance
D. Unemployment Insurance

8. The book value of a share of stock of a corporation may be found by

   A. dividing the net worth of the corporation by the number of shares of stock
   B. dividing the total amount of stock of the corporation by the number of shares of stock
   C. looking at the amount shown on the stock certificate
   D. looking at the price of the stock on the stock exchange page of the daily newspaper

9. In a business, which are MOST likely to be prepared by automatic data processing?

   A. Sales invoices
   B. Inspection reports by the night watchman
   C. Business correspondence (letters)
   D. Applications for employment

10. The entry recording the estimated depreciation for the year results in a(n) _____ in capital.

    A. increase in liabilities and a decrease
    B. decrease in liabilities and an increase
    C. increase in assets and an increase
    D. decrease in assets and a decrease

11. The balance of the Accounts Receivable controlling account would be different from the total of the Accounts Receivable Schedule if the bookkeeper

    A. made an error in totaling the Sales Journal and posted the incorrect total
    B. failed to record a sale made to S. Charles
    C. recorded the receipt of a check from a customer but neglected to record the cash discount
    D. added an invoice incorrectly and entered the incorrect total in the Sales Journal

12. Credits in the Notes Payable account USUALLY originate in the _____ Journal.

    A. Purchase   B. Cash Receipts
    C. Cash Payments   D. General

13. On the books of the seller, the deduction granted to a customer for early payment of the invoice is called a _____ discount.

    A. retail   B. purchase   C. trade   D. sales

14. A firm started the year with $25 worth of office supplies. During the year, the firm purchased $65 worth of office supplies. A count of the office supplies at the end of the year showed that $20 worth was still on hand.
    What was the TOTAL cost of the office supplies which the firm must have used during the year?

    A. $45   B. $60   C. $70   D. $110

15. A payroll check prepared by a computer is an example of _____ data processing _____.

    A. electronic; input
    B. electronic; output
    C. manual; output
    D. manual; input

16. A sale of $250 was made subject to a 7% sales tax.
    To record the sale CORRECTLY, the credits should be Sales Income

    A. $250, Sales Taxes $17.50
    B. $250, Sales Taxes Payable $17.50
    C. $267.50, Sales Taxes $17.50
    D. $267.50, Sales Taxes Payable $17.50

17. In order to determine which checks are outstanding, the bookkeeper should compare the

    A. cancelled checks with the stubs in the checkbook
    B. cancelled checks with the checks listed in the bank statement
    C. check stubs with entries made in the Cash Payments Journal
    D. checkbook deposits with entries made in the Cash Receipts Journal

18. In a sale on credit to B. Benson, the bookkeeper, by mistake, posted to the B. Boyers account.
    The error will PROBABLY be discovered when

    A. the schedule of the subsidiary ledger does not agree with the controlling account
    B. the trial balance does not balance
    C. B. Boyers receives his monthly statement
    D. the bookkeeper receives monthly statements from creditors

19. Which does a person receive as evidence of part ownership in a corporation?
    A

    A. certificate of incorporation
    B. stock certificate
    C. bond
    D. charter

20. The count of merchandise inventory on hand at the end of the year was overstated.
    This error will result in an _____ the year.

    A. *overstatement* of profit for
    B. *understatement* of profit for
    C. *overstatement* of liabilities at the end of
    D. *understatement* of assets at the end of

21. The Accounts Receivable account is an example of a _____ account.

    A. subsidiary
    B. controlling
    C. fixed asset
    D. valuation

22. The _____ check provides space for stating the purpose for which the check is written.

    A. cashier's   B. certified   C. preferred   D. voucher

23. If the assets of a firm at the end of the year were greater than the assets at the beginning of the year, then which statement would be CORRECT?

    A. The firm made a profit for the year.
    B. The firm was well managed for the year.
    C. The capital of the firm was greater at the end of the year.
    D. More information is needed before arriving at a conclusion.

24. Which is a legal characteristic of a general partnership? _____ liability.

    A. Long-term   B. Unlimited
    C. Contingent   D. Deferred

25. The term *double entry bookkeeping* means that, for each transaction, an entry is made

    A. in the journal and also in the ledger
    B. in the general ledger and also in a subsidiary ledger
    C. on the debit side of one account and on the credit side of another account
    D. on a business paper and also in the books

KEY (CORRECT ANSWERS)

1.	A	11.	A
2.	B	12.	D
3.	D	13.	D
4.	B	14.	C
5.	B	15.	B
6.	A	16.	B
7.	C	17.	A
8.	A	18.	C
9.	A	19.	B
10.	D	20.	A

21. B
22. D
23. D
24. B
25. C

EXAMINATION SECTION
TEST 1

DIRECTIONS: Each question or incomplete statement is followed by several suggested answers or completions. Select the one that BEST answers the question or completes the statement. *PRINT THE LETTER OF THE CORRECT ANSWER IN THE SPACE AT THE RIGHT.*

1. For the measurement of net income to be as realistic as possible, it is desirable that revenue be recognized at the point that

    A. cash is collected from customers
    B. an order for merchandise or services is received from a customer
    C. a deposit or advance payment is received from a customer
    D. goods are delivered or services are rendered to customers

    1.____

2. An accounting principle must receive substantial authoritative support to qualify as *generally accepted.* Many organizations and agencies have been influential in the development of generally accepted accounting principles, but the MOST influential leadership has come from the

    A. New York Stock Exchange
    B. American Institute of Certified Public Accountants
    C. Securities and Exchange Commission
    D. American Accounting Association

    2.____

3. In which one of the following ways does the declaration and payment of a cash dividend affect corporate net income?
   It _____ net income.

    A. does not affect   B. reduces
    C. increases   D. capitalizes

    3.____

4. Under which one of the following headings of the corporate balance sheet should the liability for a dividend payable in stock appear?

    A. Current Liabilities   B. Long-term Liabilities
    C. Stockholder's Equity   D. Current Assets

    4.____

5. In which one of the following is *Working Capital* MOST likely to be found?
   In

    A. Income Statement
    B. Analysis of Retained Earnings
    C. Computation of Cost of Capital
    D. Statement of Funds Provided and Applied

    5.____

6. Which of the following procedures is NOT generally mandatory in auditing a merchandising corporation?

    A. Physical observation of inventory count
    B. Written circularization of accounts receivable
    C. Confirmation of bank balance
    D. Circularization of the stockholders

    6.____

7. A company purchased office supplies in the total amount of $1,400 and charged the entire amount to the asset account. An inventory of supplies taken on December 31 shows the cost of unused supplies to be $250.
   The entry to record this fact, assuming the books have not been closed, involves

   A. credit to capital
   B. debit to supplies expense
   C. credit to supplies expense
   D. debit to supplies on hand

8. A corporation's records show $600,000 (credit) in net sales, $200,000 (debit) in year-end accounts receivable, and a $2,000 (debit) in Allowance for Bad Debts. The company's aged schedule of accounts receivable indicates a probable future loss from failure to collect year-end receivables in the amount of $6,000.
   Of the following, the MOST correct entry to adjust the Allowance for Bad Debts at year-end is

   A. $1,000 credit   B. $4,000 credit
   C. $8,000 debit   D. $8,000 credit

Questions 9-10.

DIRECTIONS: Answer Questions 9 and 10 on the basis of the information given below.

A company commenced business and purchased inventory as follows:

March	100 units	@ $5	$ 500.
June	300 units	@ 6	1,800.
October	200 units	@ 7	1,400.
November	500 units	@ 7	3,500.
December	100 units	@ 6	600.
Total	1,200		$7,800.

Units sold amounted to 900.

9. Under the LIFO inventory principle, the value of the remaining inventory is

   A. $1,700   B. $1,875   C. $2,145   D. $2,225

10. Under the FIFO inventory principle, the value of the remaining inventory is

    A. $1,650   B. $1,875   C. $2,000   D. $2,025

11. When doing a trial balance, assume that as a result of a single error, the total of the credit balances is greater than the total of the debit balances.
    Which one of the following single errors could NOT be the cause of this discrepancy?

    A. Failure to post a debit
    B. Posting a debit as a credit
    C. Failure to post a credit
    D. Posting a credit twice

Questions 12-13.

DIRECTIONS: Answer Questions 12 and 13 on the basis of the information given below.

A and B are partners with capital balances of $20,000 and $30,000 respectively at June 30, who share profits and losses 40% and 60% respectively. On July 1, C is to be admitted into the partnership under the following conditions:

Partnership assets are to be revalued and increased by $10,000.

C is to invest $40,000 but be credited for $30,000 while the remaining $10,000 is to be credited to A and B to compensate them for their pre-existing goodwill.

12. After C is admitted and the proper entries are made, A's capital account will have a credit balance of

    A. $24,500   B. $28,000   C. $30,200   D. $36,000

13. After the admission of C to the partnership, C's share of profits and losses is agreed upon at 20%.
Assuming no other adjustments, the new percentage for profit and loss distribution to A will be

    A. 18%   B. 32%   C. 36%   D. 45%

14. A company reports as income for tax purposes $70,000, and its book income before the provision for income taxes is $100,000.
Assuming a 50% tax rate, the proper tax expense to be recorded following tax allocation procedures is

    A. $33,000   B. $40,000   C. $50,000   D. $60,000

15. The relationship between the total of cash and current receivables to total current liabilities is COMMONLY referred to by accountants as the _____ ratio.

    A. acid-test   B. cross-statement
    C. current   D. R.O.I.

16. On a statement of sources and application of funds, the depreciation expense is NORMALLY shown as a(n)

    A. addition to operating income
    B. subtraction from funds provided
    C. addition to funds applied
    D. reduction from operating income

17. Company A owns 100% of the capital stock of Company B and reports on a consolidated basis. During the year, Company A sold inventory to Company B at a profit of $100,000. One-half of this inventory has been sold at year-end by Company B to the public.
Which one of the following would be the MOST correct adjustment, if any, to make the consolidated retained earnings conform to generally accepted accounting principles?

    A. Decrease by $50,000   B. Increase by $50,000
    C. Increase by $100,000   D. No adjustment

4 (#1)

18. X, Y, and Z are partners with capital of $11,000, $12,000, and $4,500. X has a loan due from the partnership to him of $2,000. Profits and losses are shared in the ratio of 4:5:1, respectively. The partnership has paid off all outside liabilities, and its remaining assets consist of $9,000 in cash and $20,500 of accounts receivable. The partners agree to disburse the $9,000 to themselves in such a way that, even if one of the receivables is realized, no partner will have been overpaid.
Under these conditions, which of the following MOST NEARLY represents the amount to be paid to partner X?

   A. $1,960   B. $3,200   C. $4,800   D. $5,000

18.____

19. R Company needs $2,000,000 to finance an expansion of plant facilities. The company expects to earn a return of 15% on this investment before considering the cost of capital or income taxes. The average income tax rate for the R Company is 40%.
If the company raises the funds by issuing 6% bonds at face value, the earnings available to common stockholders after the new plant facilities are in operation may be expected to increase by

   A. $65,000   B. $70,000   C. $108,000   D. $116,000

19.____

20. The budget for a given factory overhead cost was $150,000 for the year. The actual cost for the year was $125,000. Based on these facts, it can be said that the plant manager has done a better job than expected in controlling this cost if the cost is a

   A. semi-variable cost
   B. variable cost and actual production was 83 1/3% of budgeted production
   C. semi-variable cost which includes a fixed element of $25,000 per period
   D. variable cost and actual production was equal to budgeted production

20.____

21. The Home Office account on the books of the City Branch shows a credit balance of $15,000 at the end of a year, and the City Branch account on the books of the Home Office shows a debit balance of $12,000.
Of the following, the MOST likely reason for the discrepancy in the two accounts is that

   A. merchandise shipped by the Home Office to the branch has not been recorded by the branch
   B. the Home Office has not recorded a branch loss for the first quarter of the year
   C. the branch has just mailed a check for $3,000 to the Home Office which has not yet been received by the Home Office
   D. the Home Office has not yet recorded the branch profit for the first quarter of the year

21.____

22. The concept of matching costs and revenues means that

   A. the expenses offset against revenues should be related to the same time period
   B. revenues are at least as great as expenses on the average
   C. revenues and expenses are equal
   D. net income equals revenues minus expenses for the same earning period

22.____

23. If the inventory at the end of the current year is understated and the error is not caught during the following year, the effect is to

   A. overstate the income for the two-year period
   B. overstate income this year and understate income next year

23.____

C. understate income this year and overstate income next year
D. understate income this year, with no effect on the income of the next year

Questions 24-25.

DIRECTIONS: Answer Questions 24 and 25 on the basis of the information given below.

Investment Account

Date	Explanation	Shares	Amount	Date	Explanation	Shares	Amount
1/7/15	Cash purchase	250	$27,000	2016	Cash dividends		$5,000
12/1/17	2-for-1 split	250	$27,000*	4/15/17	Proceeds of sale	125	26,000
		Total	$54,000	12/31/17	Balance	375	23,000
1/1/18	Balance	375	$23,000			Total	$54,000

*This amount is a result of the following entry:
 Debit - Investment Account $27,000
   Credit - Investment Income $27,000

In addition to the above information, you are informed that a stock dividend of 225 shares was received on January 1, 2017 but had not been recorded. All of these transactions are related to the investment in stock of the same corporation.

24. The CORRECT dollar balance of the investment account on December 31, 2017 should be   24._____

 A. $12,000   B. $18,000   C. $22,000   D. $24,000

25. The CORRECT number of shares owned on December 31, 2017 was   25._____

 A. 425   B. 500   C. 575   D. 675

26. During a period of rising prices, the inventory pricing method which might be expected to give the LOWEST net income on the income statement is   26._____

 A. FIFO
 B. LIFO
 C. Weighted-average cost
 D. Lower of Cost or Market (cost on a FIFO basis)

27. Carteret Corporation bought land for $100,000. The land was subject to delinquent property taxes of $6,900. The Carteret Corporation immediately paid these delinquent taxes and also paid interest charges and penalties in the amount of $625 related to the delinquent taxes. The land was immediately placed in use as a parking lot. During the first year of use, the property taxes amounted to $1,800.   27._____
The cost of the land should be recorded on the books as

 A. $102,525   B. $105,400   C. $107,525   D. $108,525

28. Which of the following series of accounts are among those that will appear on a statement of Cost of Goods Manufactured?

    A. Freight-in on raw materials, ending inventory of goods in process, indirect labor, purchase discounts on raw materials
    B. Goods in process inventory, factory supplies used, sales of manufactured goods, property tax expense
    C. Raw materials purchased, finished goods inventory, depreciation on factory machinery
    D. Direct labor, sales commission on manufactured products, factory building occupancy costs

29. Standard costing will produce the same cost of goods sold as actual costing when the cost variances are

    A. treated as income or expense items
    B. allocated to the Cost of Goods Sold and ending inventories
    C. reported in the Balance Sheet as a deferred charge or deferred credit
    D. closed to Cost of Goods Sold account

30. A job-order cost system would be appropriate in the manufacture of

    A. paints
    B. custom-made furniture
    C. breakfast cereals
    D. standard grade of plywood

KEY (CORRECT ANSWERS)

1.	D	16.	A
2.	B	17.	A
3.	A	18.	C
4.	C	19.	C
5.	D	20.	D
6.	D	21.	D
7.	B	22.	A
8.	D	23.	C
9.	A	24.	B
10.	C	25.	B
11.	C	26.	B
12.	B	27.	C
13.	B	28.	A
14.	C	29.	B
15.	A	30.	B

EXAMINATION SECTION
TEST 1

DIRECTIONS: Each question or incomplete statement is followed by several suggested answers or completions. Select the one that BEST answers the question or completes the statement. *PRINT THE LETTER OF THE CORRECT ANSWER IN THE SPACE AT THE RIGHT.*

Questions 1-7.

DIRECTIONS: Questions 1 through 7 are to be answered on the basis of the following income statement.

    Laura Lee's Bridal Shop
    Income Statement
    For the Year Ended December 31, 2018

Revenue:		
New & Used Bridal Gowns & Accessories		$55,000
Expenses:		
Advertisement Expense	$ 2,000	
Salaries Expense	12,000	
Dry cleaning & Alterations	10,000	
Utilities	1,500	
Total Expenses		25,500
Net Income		$29,500

1. What is the period of time covered by this income statement?   1.____

   A. January-December 2017
   B. December 2018
   C. January 2017-December 2018
   D. January-December 2018

2. What is the source of the revenue?   2.____

   A. New and used bridal gowns, advertisements, salaries, dry cleaning, and utilities
   B. Advertisements, salaries, dry cleaning, alterations, and utilities
   C. New and used bridal gowns and accessories
   D. Net income

3. What is the total revenue?   3.____

   A. $25,500   B. $55,000   C. $29,500   D. $79,500

4. Which of the following are expenses?   4.____

   A. Salaries
   B. New and used bridal gowns and accessories
   C. Revenue
   D. New and used bridal gowns, advertisements, and dry cleaning

5. What are the total expenses?   5.____

   A. $55,000   B. $29,500   C. $79,500   D. $25,500

2 (#1)

6. There is a resulting net income because 6.____

   A. total revenue and total expenses are combined
   B. net income is greater than total revenue
   C. the total revenue is greater than total expenses
   D. the total revenue is less than total expenses

7. Is this statement an interim statement? 7.____

   A. Yes, because it covers an entire accounting period
   B. No, because it covers an entire accounting period
   C. Yes, because it covers a period of less than a year
   D. No, because it covers a period of more than a year

8. What is the name of the accounting report that may show either a net profit or a net loss for an accounting period? 8.____

   A. Income statement   B. Balance sheet
   C. Statement of capital   D. Classified balance sheet

9. What are the two main parts of the body of the income statement? 9.____

   A. Cash and Capital   B. Revenue and Expenses
   C. Liabilities and Capital   D. Assets and Notes Payable

10. If total revenue exceeds total expenses for an accounting period, what is the difference called? 10.____

    A. Gross income   B. Total liabilities
    C. Total assets   D. Net income

11. In the body of a balance sheet, what are the three sections called? 11.____

    A. Assets and liabilities
    B. Cash, liabilities, and revenue
    C. Assets, liabilities, and capital
    D. Revenue, assets, and capital

12. What business record shows the results of the proprietor's borrowing assets from the business, usually in anticipation of profits? 12.____

    A. Proprietor's withdrawals
    B. Accounts payable
    C. Liabilities and Capital
    D. Total liabilities

Questions 13-24.

DIRECTIONS: For each transaction given for Mona's Magic Moments Hair Salon in Questions 13 through 24, identify which journal the transaction should be recorded in.

13. April 1: Mona, the owner, paid the month's rent - $600.00; check no. 356. 13.____

    A. General   B. Cash disbursements
    C. Purchases   D. Sales

14. April 6: the salon purchased $300.00 worth of styling products on account from Pomme de Terre Company.   14.____

    A. Cash disbursements   B. General
    C. Sales   D. Purchases

15. April 8: sold $100.00 worth of hair products on account to Mrs. Angela Bray.   15.____

    A. Sales   B. Purchases
    C. Cash disbursements   D. General

16. April 11: the owner, Mona Ramen, withdrew $80.00 of styling products for personal use.   16.____

    A. Sales   B. Cash receipts
    C. General   D. Cash disbursements

17. April 13: paid Pomme de Terre Company $300.00 on account; check 357.   17.____

    A. Purchases   B. Cash disbursements
    C. Cash receipts   D. General

18. April 15: cash sales to date were $4,607.00.   18.____

    A. Cash disbursements   B. Purchases
    C. Sales   D. General

19. April 17: issued credit slip #17 to Mrs. Angela Bray for $25.00 for merchandise returned.   19.____

    A. Cash disbursements   B. Cash receipts
    C. Sales   D. General

20. April 19: paid electric bill for $250.00; check no. 358.   20.____

    A. Cash disbursements   B. Purchases
    C. General   D. Cash receipts

21. April 21: received $75.00 from Mrs. Angela Bray for balance due on account.   21.____

    A. Sales   B. Cash disbursements
    C. Cash receipts   D. Purchases

22. April 23: sold $88.00 of hair products on account to Ms. Tania Alioto.   22.____

    A. Purchases   B. Sales
    C. Cash disbursements   D. Cash receipts

23. April 27: purchased $500.00 of equipment from Salon Stylings Merchandisers on account.   23.____

    A. Cash disbursements   B. Sales
    C. General   D. Purchases

24. April 30: cash sales to date were $5023.00.   24.____

    A. Purchases   B. Sales
    C. Cash receipts   D. General

Questions 25-30.

DIRECTIONS: Questions 25 through 30 are to be answered on the basis of the following ledger for a barbecue take-out restaurant owned and operated by Ruby Joiner.

Cash		Accounts Receivable		Delivery Equipment	
450	150	360	170	5,000	
212	125	250	100	4,000	
328	440	165	120	3,000	
172	125	100	60		
250	70				
275	150				
325	50				

Supplies		Ruby Joiner, Capital		Accounts Payable	
40			8,200	10	600
65			2,000	15	300
30			2,097		200
25					

Ruby Joiner, Drawing		Advertising Expense		Delivery Income	
225		40			400
175		45			350
200					250
					100

Trucking Expense		Telephone Expense	
100		80	
50		40	
		20	

25. What is the balance on the Cash account shown above?

    A. 2,012.00   B. 1,110.00   C. 3,122.00   D. 902.00

26. What is the balance on the Accounts receivable account shown above?

    A. 425.00   B. 875.00   C. 450.00   D. 1315.00

27. What is the balance on the Accounts payable account shown above?

    A. 1100.00   B. 1075.00   C. 25.00   D. 1125.00

28. Which of the above accounts has a balance of 1100.00?

    A. Accounts payable   B. Delivery Income
    C. Cash   D. Delivery equipment

29. Which of the above accounts has a balance of 12,000.00?

    A. Ruby Joiner, Capital
    B. Cash and Accounts receivable combined
    C. Delivery equipment
    D. None of the accounts

30. If you made a balance sheet out of the information listed above, Ruby Joiner's total assets would be

    A. 14,472.00   B. 12,297.00   C. 13,392.00   D. 13,487.00

Questions 31-34.

DIRECTIONS: Questions 31 through 34 are to be answered on the basis of the following information, to be included on a checking deposit ticket.

Five $20 bills; 11 $10 bills; 6 $5 bills; 47 $1 bills; 200 half dollars; 120 quarters; 112 dimes; 320 nickels; 67 pennies. Second National Bank (73-124) check of 152.34; Bank of the Midwest (13-298) check of 68.37; Great National Bank (32-165) check of 185.06.

31. What is the TOTAL currency for this deposit? 31._____
   A. $387 B. $287 C. $444.87 D. $157.87

32. What is the TOTAL coin for this deposit? 32._____
   A. $387 B. $287 C. $444.87 D. $157.87

33. What is the check total for this deposit? 33._____
   A. $692.77 B. $406 C. $405.77 D. $850.64

34. What is the TOTAL deposit? 34._____
   A. $444.87 B. $692.77 C. $851 D. $850.64

Questions 35-37.

DIRECTIONS: Questions 35 through 37 are to be answered on the basis of the following petty cash journal.

Date	Receipt No.	To Whom Paid	For What	Acct.#	Amount
10/2	1	Anna Jones - Mail	Postage	548	13.50
10/2	2	Jim Collins	Messenger	525	5.75
10/4	3	Anna Jones - Mail	Postage	548	13.50
10/5	4	Lucky Stores	Coffee	515	7.34
10/6	5	Tom Allen	Lunch w/customer	525	11.38

35. What is the TOTAL disbursement from this fund for the time period 10/1 through 10/6? 35._____
   A. $51.47 B. $40.09 C. $61.47 D. $26.59

36. How much money was disbursed to Account #548 during the time period 10/1-10/16? 36._____
   A. $51.47 B. $26 C. $27 D. $34.34

37. If the fund began the month with a total of $100.00, what amount was left in the fund at the end of business on 10/5? 37._____
   A. $48.53 B. $59.91 C. $51.47 D. $40.09

Questions 38-40.

DIRECTIONS: Questions 38 through 40 are to be answered on the basis of the following information.

A promissory note dated December 1, 2018, bearing interest at a rate of 12% and due in 90 days, is sent to a creditor. The face value of the note is $900.

38. What is the due date of the promissory note? 38.____
   A. January 15, 2019
   B. March 1, 2019
   C. February 1, 2019
   D. December 31, 2018

39. What is the TOTAL interest that will be earned on the note? 39.____
   A. $27
   B. $270
   C. $108
   D. $10.80

40. What interest will be earned on the note for the old accounting period (December 1-31)? 40.____
   A. $90
   B. $36
   C. $9
   D. $3.60

KEY (CORRECT ANSWERS)

1.	D	11.	C	21.	C	31.	B
2.	C	12.	A	22.	B	32.	D
3.	B	13.	B	23.	D	33.	C
4.	A	14.	D	24.	B	34.	D
5.	D	15.	A	25.	D	35.	A
6.	C	16.	C	26.	A	36.	C
7.	B	17.	B	27.	B	37.	B
8.	A	18.	C	28.	B	38.	B
9.	B	19.	D	29.	C	39.	A
10.	D	20.	A	30.	D	40.	C

TEST 2

DIRECTIONS: Each question or incomplete statement is followed by several suggested answers or completions. Select the one that BEST answers the question or completes the statement. *PRINT THE LETTER OF THE CORRECT ANSWER IN THE SPACE AT THE RIGHT.*

Questions 1-4.

DIRECTIONS: Questions 1 through 4 are to be answered on the basis of the following information, to be included in a deposit slip.

    14 twenty dollar bills   63 quarters
    52 ten dollar bills   22 dimes
    12 five dollar bills   44 nickels
    43 one dollar bills   70 pennies

Checks: $236.34 and $129.72

1. What is the TOTAL amount of currency for this deposit?   1.____

    A. $923.85   B. $1269.06   C. $903.00   D. $1299.91

2. What is the TOTAL amount of coin for this deposit?   2.____

    A. $20.85   B. $923.85   C. $903.00   D. $1299.91

3. What is the TOTAL amount of check for this deposit?   3.____

    A. $20.85   B. $366.06   C. $1299.91   D. $903.00

4. What is the TOTAL deposit for this slip?   4.____

    A. $1269.06   B. $903.00   C. $923.85   D. $1289.91

Questions 5-7.

DIRECTIONS: Questions 5 through 7 are to be answered on the basis of the following information.

Angela Martinez's last check stub balance was $675.50. Her bank statement balance dated April 30 was $652.00. A $250 deposit was in transit on that date. Outstanding checks were as follows: No. 127, $65.00; No. 129, $203.50; No. 130, $50.00. The bank service charge for the month was $5.00.

5. What was Angela Martinez's available checkbook balance on April 30?   5.____

    A. $652.00   B. $338.50   C. $583.50   D. $675.50

6. In order to reconcile her checkbook balance with her bank statement balance, what must Angela Martinez do?   6.____

    A. Add her checkbook balance to the balance on her bank statement
    B. Subtract her checkbook balance from the balance on her bank statement

C. Ignore her checkbook balance and adopt the balance on her bank statement
D. Adjust the checkbook balance by adding deposits and debiting outstanding checks and charges

7. The check stub balance referred to in the problem refers to the 7._____

   A. last check Angela Martinez recorded in her checkbook
   B. amount of money left in Angela Martinez's account according to her own calculations based on the checks, charges, and deposits she has written and recorded
   C. amount of money left in Angela Martinez's account according to the bank's calculations based on the checks, charges, and deposits posted to her account
   D. number of checks left in her checkbook

Questions 8-9.

DIRECTIONS: Questions 8 and 9 are to be answered on the basis of the following information.

Tu Nguyen, an interior designer, received his June bank statement on July 2. The balance was $622.66. His last check stub balance was $700. On comparing the two, he noticed that a deposit of $275 made on June 30 was not included on the statement; also, a bank service charge of $4 was deducted. Outstanding checks were as follows: No. 331, $97.50; No. 332, $207; No. 335, $25.40; and No. 336, $68.97.

8. What is Nguyen's CORRECT available bank balance? 8._____

   A. $494.79   B. $897.66   C. $700.00   D. $219.79

9. The bank statement balance referred to in the problem refers to the 9._____

   A. last check Tu Nguyen recorded in his checkbook
   B. last check presented for payment to Tu Nguyen's account
   C. amount of money left in Tu Nguyen's account according to the bank's calculations based on the checks, charges, and deposits posted to his account
   D. amount of money left in Tu Nguyen's account based on his own calculations of the checks, charges, and deposits he has written and recorded

10. What of the following endorsements would be an example of a simple Endorsement in Blank? 10._____

    A. Pay to the Order of Joanie Anderson
    B. Joanie Anderson
    C. For deposit only; Acct. No. 12345; Joanie Anderson
    D. Without Recourse; Joanie Anderson

11. Which of the following endorsements would limit the further purpose or use of the endorsed check? 11._____

    A. Pay to the Order of Joanie Anderson
    B. Joanie Anderson
    C. For deposit only; Acct. No. 12345; Joanie Anderson,
    D. Without Recourse; Joanie Anderson

12. Which of the following endorsements would protect the endorser from legal responsibility for payment, should the drawer have insufficient funds to honor his/her own check? 12._____

    A. Pay to the Order of Joanie Anderson
    B. Joanie Anderson
    C. For deposit only; Acct. No. 12345; Joanie Anderson
    D. Without Recourse; Joanie Anderson

Questions 13-24.

DIRECTIONS: Questions 13 - 24 are to be answered on the basis of the following ledger accounts for Wheelsmith Organic Farms.

Wheelsmith Organic Farms
Ledger Accounts

Cash	Accounts Payable	Service Supplies
Jan. 1 4,000	Jan. 1 2,000	Jan. 1 2,000

Shelley Wheelsmith, Capital	Machinery
Jan. 1 11,000	Jan. 1 7,000

13. Transaction #1: On January 5, Shelley Wheelsmith, the proprietor, received cash amounting to $5,000 as a result of returning machinery that had recently been purchased. What account(s) should this transaction be posted to? 13._____

    A. Cash
    B. Cash and Machinery
    C. Machinery
    D. Cash, Machinery, and Service Supplies

14. Transaction #2: On January 8, Shelley Wheelsmith, the proprietor, sent out a check for $600 in partial payment of the accounts payable.
    What account(s) should this transaction be posted to? 14._____

    A. Accounts Payable
    B. Accounts Payable and Cash
    C. Accounts Payable and Capital
    D. Cash

15. Transaction #3: On January 14, Shelley Wheelsmith, proprietor, made an additional investment in the business by contributing machinery valued at $1,500.
    What account(s) should this transaction be posted to? 15._____

    A. Machinery   B. Machinery and Capital
    C. Capital   D. Machinery and Cash

16. Transaction #4: On January 26, Shelley Wheelsmith, proprietor, purchased additional service supplies for $200. She agreed to pay the obligation in 30 days. What account(s) should this transaction be posted to? 16._____

A. Accounts Payable and Liabilities
B. Service supplies
C. Accounts Payable
D. Accounts Payable and Service supplies

17. Transaction #5: On January 31, Shelley Wheelsmith, proprietor, purchased service supplies paying cash of $50. What account(s) should this transaction be posted to?   17.____

   A. Service supplies
   B. Service supplies and Accounts Payable
   C. Cash and Service supplies
   D. Cash

18. What is the balance in the Cash account after all of these transactions are posted?   18.____

   A. $9,000   B. $1,000   C. $5,000   D. $8,350

19. What is the balance in the Machinery account after all of these transactions are posted?   19.____

   A. $7,000   B. $5,000   C. $3,500   D. $13,500

20. What is the balance in the Accounts Payable account after all of these transactions are posted?   20.____

   A. $800   B. $600   C. $2,600   D. $1,600

21. What is the balance in the Capital account after all of these transactions are posted?   21.____

   A. $12,500   B. $800   C. $11,600   D. $10,400

22. What is the balance in the Service supplies account after all of these transactions are posted?   22.____

   A. $2,000   B. $2,250   C. $750   D. $2,200

23. What are the total assets of Wheelsmith Organic Farms after these transactions have been posted?   23.____

   A. $10,600   B. $11,850   C. $14,100   D. $10,750

24. What are the total liabilities and capital for Wheelsmith Organic Farms after these transactions have been posted?   24.____

   A. $14,100   B. $12,500   C. $11,850   D. $10,600

Questions 25-28.

DIRECTIONS: Questions 25 through 28 are to be answered on the basis of the following information.

At the end of an accounting period, Andy's Framing Gallery recorded the following information: Sales, $125,225; Merchandise Inventory, December 31, $95,325; Purchases Returns and Allowances, $3,500; Merchandise Inventory, January 1, $98,725; Freight on Purchases, $2,500; Purchases, $120,000.

25. What are the net purchases for Andy's Framing Gallery during the accounting period? 25.____
    A. $120,000   B. $119,000   C. $3,500   D. $122,500

26. What is the cost of goods available for sale? 26.____
    A. $119,000   B. $98,725   C. $95,325   D. $217,725

27. What is the total cost of goods sold for this accounting period? 27.____
    A. $217,725   B. $95,325   C. $122,400   D. $125,225

28. What is the gross profit on sales for this accounting period? 28.____
    A. $2825   B. $2500   C. $125,225   D. $122,400

Questions 29-40.

DIRECTIONS: Questions 29 through 40 are to be answered on the basis of the following information.

The Joie de Vivre Co. received the promissory notes listed below during the last quarter of its calendar year:

	Date	Face Amount	Terms	Interest Rate	Date Discounted	Discount Rate
(1)	10/8	$3,600	30 days	-	10/18	9%
(2)	9/22	$8,000	60 days	6%	10/1	7%
(3)	11/15	$3,000	90 days	7%	11/20	8%

29. What is the due date for the first note? 29.____
    A. 12/31   B. 11/7   C. 12/7   D. 10/31

30. What interest will be due when the first note matures? 30.____
    A. $3   B. $3,600   C. $30   D. $0

31. What is the maturity value of the first note? 31.____
    A. $3,600   B. $3,630   C. $0   D. $3,603

32. What is the discount period for the first note? 32.____
    A. One fiscal year   B. 10 days
    C. 20 days   D. One month

33. What is the due date for the second note? 33.____
    A. 12/21   B. 11/21   C. 10/21   D. 1/21

34. What interest will be due when the second note matures? 34.____
    A. $60   B. $800.00   C. $8.00   D. $80.00

35. What is the maturity value of the second note? 35.____
    A. $8,000   B. $8,080   C. $8,800   D. $8,008

36. What is the discount period for the second note?   36._____
    A. 51 days   B. 10 days   C. 360 days   D. 60 days

37. What is the due date for the third note?   37._____
    A. 1/14   B. 12/15   C. 12/31   D. 2/13

38. What interest will be due when the third note matures?   38._____
    A. $5.25   B. $52.50   C. $525   D. $90

39. What is the maturity value of the third note?   39._____
    A. $3525   B. $3005.25   C. $3052.50   D. $3090

40. What is the discount period for the third note?   40._____
    A. 60 days   B. 85 days   C. 5 days   D. 90 days

KEY (CORRECT ANSWERS)

1.	C	11.	C	21.	A	31.	A
2.	A	12.	D	22.	B	32.	C
3.	B	13.	B	23.	C	33.	B
4.	D	14.	B	24.	A	34.	D
5.	C	15.	B	25.	B	35.	B
6.	D	16.	D	26.	D	36.	A
7.	B	17.	C	27.	C	37.	D
8.	A	18.	D	28.	A	38.	B
9.	C	19.	C	29.	B	39.	C
10.	B	20.	D	30.	D	40.	B

TEST 3

DIRECTIONS: Each question or incomplete statement is followed by several suggested answers or completions. Select the one that BEST answers the question or completes the statement. *PRINT THE LETTER OF THE CORRECT ANSWER IN THE SPACE AT THE RIGHT.*

Questions 1-8.

DIRECTIONS: Questions 1 through 8 are to be answered on the basis of the following Balance Sheet.

Laura Lee's Bridal Shop
Balance Sheet
December 31, 2018

Assets

Cash	$14,000	
Accounts Receivable	3,000	
Bridal Accessories	10,000	
Gowns and Other Inventory	30,000	
Total Assets		$57,000

Liabilities and Capital

Accounts Payable	$ 4,000	
Notes Payable	28,000	
Total Liabilities		$32,000
Laura Lee, Capital		25,000
Total Liabilities and Capital		$57,000

1. When was the balance sheet prepared?　　　　　　　　　　　　　　　　　　　　　　　　　　　　1.____

   A. January 2019
   B. December 31, 2018
   C. After the close of the 2018 fiscal year
   D. December 1, 2018

2. How does the date on this balance sheet differ from the date on the statement of capital　2.____
   or income statement?

   A. It doesn't differ. The dates for each statement signify the same time period.
   B. The date on a balance sheet represents the period during which any changes indicated on the statement took place, whereas the other financial statements represent the moment in time when the statement was prepared.
   C. The date on a balance sheet represents the moment in time when the statement was prepared, whereas the other financial statements represent the period during which any changes indicated on the statement took place.
   D. The date on a balance sheet indicates an entire year, whereas the dates on the other statements indicate a single month.

3. Can Laura Lee purchase more bridal gowns for the business paying cash of $16,000?　　3.____

   A. No, because the business has only $14,000 cash available
   B. Yes, because the business has $57,000 cash available
   C. Yes, because the business has $57,000 available in assets
   D. No, because the business has $57,000 in liabilities

65

4. What is the owner's equity of Laura Lee's Bridal Shop?   4._____
   Since total equity consists of total _____, total equity is _____.

   A. assets minus total liabilities and proprietor's capital; $0
   B. assets minus total liabilities; $25,000
   C. assets; $57,000
   D. liabilities and proprietor's capital; $57,000

5. What is the TOTAL amount of Laura Lee's claim against the total assets of the business?   5._____

   A. $57,000   B. $25,000   C. $0   D. $39,000

6. What is the amount of the creditors' claims against the assets of the business?   6._____

   A. $4,000   B. $57,000   C. $32,000   D. $28,000

7. What is the net income for the period?   7._____

   A. $57,000
   B. $0
   C. $25,000
   D. This information cannot be obtained from the balance sheet

8. What was the value of Laura Lee's ownership in this business on January 1, 2004?   8._____

   A. $25,000
   B. $57,000
   C. $14,000
   D. This information cannot be obtained from the balance sheet

Questions 9-21.

DIRECTIONS: Each of the transactions described in Questions 9 through 21 occurred within an accounting period. For each question, indicate which of the four journals the transaction would be recorded in.

9. Sale of goods on account   9._____

   A. Cash receipts   B. Cash payments
   C. General   D. Sales

10. Cash payment of a promissory note   10._____

    A. Cash payments   B. Cash receipts
    C. Sales   D. General

11. Received a credit memo from a creditor   11._____

    A. Purchases   B. General
    C. Sales   D. Cash payments

12. Sale of merchandise for cash   12._____

    A. Purchases   B. General
    C. Cash receipts   D. Cash payments

13. Received a check from a customer in partial payment of an oral agreement   13._____

    A. Purchases   B. Sales
    C. General   D. Cash receipts

14. Issued a credit memo to a customer   14._____

    A. Purchases   B. General
    C. Cash payments   D. Sales

15. Received a promissory note in place of an oral agreement from a customer   15._____

    A. General   B. Cash payments
    C. Cash receipts   D. Sales

16. Paid monthly rent   16._____

    A. General   B. Purchases
    C. Cash payments   D. Cash receipts

17. Sale of a service on credit   17._____

    A. Cash receipts   B. General
    C. Purchases   D. Sales

18. Purchase of office furniture on credit   18._____

    A. General   B. Purchases
    C. Cash payments   D. Cash receipts

19. Purchased merchandise for cash   19._____

    A. Cash payments   B. Cash receipts
    C. Sales   D. General

20. Cash refund to a customer   20._____

    A. Cash receipts   B. Sales
    C. General   D. Cash payments

21. Purchases made on credit   21._____

    A. Purchases   B. Sales
    C. Cash receipts   D. General

Questions 22-26.

DIRECTIONS: Questions 22 through 26 are to be answered on the basis of the following inventory, purchased by International Soap and Candle Traders, Inc.

700 units at $4.50, 320 units at $3.75, 550 units at $2.75, and 475 units at $1.90

22. Calculate the total price of the units that cost $4.50.   22._____

    A. $315   B. $31,500   C. $3,150   D. $2,800

23. Calculate the total price of the units that cost $3.75.   23._____

    A. $2062.50   B. $12,000   C. $120   D. $1,200

24. Calculate the total price of the units that cost $2.75. 24.____

    A. $1,512.50   B. $15,125   C. $151.25   D. $550

25. Calculate the total price of the units that cost $1.90. 25.____

    A. $90.25   B. $9025   C. $902.50   D. $475

26. Calculate the average cost per unit. 26.____

    A. $27   B. $33.10   C. $0.30   D. $3.31

27. The interest on a promissory note is recorded at which of the following times? 27.____

    A. When the debt is incurred
    B. At the end of the accounting period
    C. When the note is paid
    D. At the beginning of each month

28. The interest on a promissory note begins accruing at which of the following times? 28.____

    A. When the debt is incurred
    B. At the end of the accounting period
    C. When the note is paid
    D. At the beginning of each month

29. The maturity value of an interest-bearing note is the 29.____

    A. interest accrued on the note plus a service charge imposed by the lender
    B. interest accrued on the note
    C. face value of the note
    D. principal of the note plus interest

30. A cash receipts journal is used to record the 30.____

    A. number of cash sales a business makes
    B. number of credit sales a business makes
    C. collection of cash made by the business
    D. expenditure of cash made by the business

31. Calculate the interest on a promissory note issued for $3,000 at an interest rate of 8%, due in 360 days. (Assume a banking year of 360 days.) 31.____

    A. $300   B. $240   C. $60   D. $360

32. Calculate the total payment due for a promissory note issued for $1,000 at an interest rate of 10%, due in 90 days. (Assume a banking year of 360 days.) 32.____

    A. $25   B. $1050   C. $1000   D. $1025

33. Calculate the total payment due for a promissory note issued for $5,000 at an interest rate of 6%, due in 60 days. (Assume a banking year of 360 days.) 33.____

    A. $5,050   B. $50   C. $5,000   D. $5,300

34. Calculate the interest on a promissory note issued for $1,700 at an interest rate of 12%, due in 45 days. (Assume a banking year of 360 days.)   34.____

    A. $204   B. $1725.50   C. $25.50   D. $1904

35. Calculate the interest on a promissory note issued for $600 at an interest rate of 9%, due in 90 days. (Assume a banking year of 360 days.)   35.____

    A. $13.50   B. $135   C. $54   D. $540

KEY (CORRECT ANSWERS)

1.	B	16.	C
2.	C	17.	D
3.	A	18.	B
4.	B	19.	A
5.	B	20.	D
6.	C	21.	A
7.	D	22.	C
8.	D	23.	D
9.	D	24.	A
10.	A	25.	C
11.	B	26.	D
12.	C	27.	C
13.	D	28.	A
14.	B	29.	D
15.	A	30.	C

31. B
32. D
33. A
34. C
35. A

EXAMINATION SECTION
TEST 1

DIRECTIONS: Each question or incomplete statement is followed by several suggested answers or completions. Select the one that BEST answers the question or completes the statement. *PRINT THE LETTER OF THE CORRECT ANSWER IN THE SPACE AT THE RIGHT.*

Questions 1-5.

DIRECTIONS: Questions 1 through 5 are to be answered on the basis of the following information.

Assume that you are working in an agency and that you are requested to verify certain financial data with respect to the various business entities described below. This information is required to verify that tax returns and/or other financial reports submitted to your agency are correct.

In an auditing review of the income statements of several business firms (Companies X, Y, and Z), you find the financial information given below. Based upon the account balances shown, select the correct answer for the statement information requested.

1. Company X
   Sales $ 160,000
   Opening inventory $ 70,000
   Purchases $ 80,000
   Purchase returns $ 1,200
   Cost of goods sold $ 127,000
   The ending inventory based upon the above data is

   A. $21,800   B. $23,000   C. $24,200   D. $33,000

2. Company Y
   Opening inventory $ 50,000
   Purchases $ 145,000
   Ending inventory $ 28,500
   Gross profit $ 56,000
   Sales and administrative expenses $ 64,000
   Sales for the period based upon the above data are

   A. $110,500   B. $166,500   C. $222,500   D. $286,500

3. Company Z
   Sales for the period $ 200,000
   Net profit   7% of sales
   Purchases $ 180,000
   Ending inventory $ 70,000
   Gross profit $ 60,000
   Cost of goods sold for Company Z is

   A. $110,000   B. $140,000   C. $180,000   D. $250,000

4. The opening inventory of Company Z would be

   A. $10,000   B. $20,000   C. $30,000   D. $80,000

5. The operating expenses for Company Z would be

   A. $10,000   B. $14,000   C. $20,000   D. $46,000

Questions 6-8.

DIRECTIONS: Questions 6 through 8 are to be answered on the basis of the following information, which is taken from the books and records of a business firm.

Sales for the calendar year	$52,000
Based upon FIFO Inventory:	
Goods available for sale	$46,900
Inventory at December 31	$12,700
Based upon LIFO Inventory:	
Goods available for sale	$46,900
Inventory at December 31	$10,400

6. If FIFO Inventory valuation is used, the gross profit will be

   A. $5,100   B. $15,500   C. $17,800   D. $34,200

7. If LIFO Inventory valuation method is used, the gross profit will be

   A. $2,300   B. $15,500   C. $17,800   D. $36,500

8. If LIFO Inventory method is used, compared with the FIFO method, the cost of goods sold will be

   A. more by $2,300   B. less by $2,300
   C. more by $10,400   D. less by $12,700

9. Which one of the following would NOT properly be classified as an asset on the balance sheet of a business firm?

   A. Investment in stock of another firm
   B. Premium cost of a three-year fire insurance policy
   C. Cash surrender value of life insurance on life of corporate officer; policy is owned by the company and the company is the beneficiary
   D. Amounts owing to employees for services rendered

10. Which one of the following would NOT properly be classified as a current asset?

    A. Travel advances to salespeople
    B. Postage in a postage meter
    C. Cash surrender value of life insurance policy on an officer which policy names the corporation as the beneficiary
    D. Installment notes receivable due over 18 months in accordance with normal trade practice

11. Able, Baker, and Carr formed a partnership. Able contributed $10,000; Baker contributed $5,000; and Carr contributed an automobile with a fair market value of $5,000. They have no partnership agreement. The first year, the partnership earned $18,000. The partners will share the profits as follows: Able, _____; Baker, _____; Carr, _____.

    A. $9,000; $4,500; $4,500
    B. $6,000; $6,000; $6,000
    C. $12,000; $6,000; no share
    D. $8,000; $5,000; $5,000

11.____

Questions 12-13.

DIRECTIONS: Questions 12 and 13 are to be answered on the basis of the information below.

The XYZ partnership had the following balance sheet as of December 31:

Cash	$ 5,000
Other assets	40,000
Total	$45,000
Liabilities	$12,000
X Capital	20,000
Y Capital	10,000
Z Capital	3,000
Total	$45,000

The partners shared profits equally. They decided to liquidate the partnership at December 31.

12. If the other assets were sold for $52,000, each partner will be entitled to a final cash distribution of:
    X, _____; Y, _____; Z, _____.

    A. $15,000; $15,000; $15,000
    B. $24,000; $14,000; $7,000
    C. $20,000; $10,000; $3,000
    D. $23,000; $13,000; $6,000

12.____

13. If the other assets were sold for $31,000, each partner will be entitled to a final cash distribution of:
    X, _____; Y, _____; Z, _____.

    A. $14,000; $5,000; $5,000
    B. $8,000; $8,000; $8,000
    C. $15,000; $15,000; $15,000
    D. $17,000; $7,000; no cash share

13.____

14. Items selling for $40 for which there were 10% selling costs were purchased for inventory at $20 each. Selling prices and costs remained steady, but at the date of the financial statement the market price had dropped to $16. The inventory remaining from the original purchase was written down to $16.
Of the following, it is CORRECT to state that the _____ overstated.

   A. cost of sales of the subsequent year will be
   B. current year's income is
   C. income of the following year will be
   D. closing inventory of the current year is

15. Dividends in arrears on a cumulative preferred stock should be reported on the balance sheet as

   A. an accrued liability
   B. restricted retained earnings
   C. an explanatory note
   D. a deduction from preferred stock

16. The effect of recording the payment of a 10% dividend paid in stock would be to

   A. *increase* the current ratio
   B. *decrease* the amount of working capital
   C. *increase* the total stockholder equity
   D. *decrease* the book value per share of stock outstanding

17. The owner of a truck which originally had cost $12,000 but now has a book value of $1,500 was offered $3,000 for it by a used truck dealer. However, the owner traded it in for a new truck listed at $19,000 and received a trade-in allowance of $4,000.
The cost basis for the new truck following the Federal income tax rules properly amounts to

   A. $15,000   B. $16,000   C. $16,500   D. $17,500

18. In planning for purchases to be made during the next month, the following information is to be used:

   Budgeted sales for the month   73,000 units
   Inventory at beginning of the month   19,000 units
   Planned inventory at end of the month 14,000 units

   From the above information, the amount of units to be purchased is _____ units.

   A. 40,000   B. 59,000   C. 68,000   D. 78,000

19. A branch office of a company has the following plan:

   Cash balance at beginning of the month $ 10,000
   Planned cash balance at end of the month $ 15,000
   Expected receipts for the month $ 180,000
   Expected disbursements for the month $ 205,000

   In order to comply with this plan, the accountant should recommend that the branch obtain an additional allocation of

   A. $20,000   B. $25,000   C. $30,000   D. $50,000

20. A company uses the reserve method of bad debt expense and sets up a bad debt account at 2% of sales. The sales were $500,000. The company wrote off $7,500 in accounts receivable.
The effect of these entries on net income for the period is a(n)

A. $2,500 increase
C. $8,000 decrease
B. $7,500 decrease
D. $10,000 decrease

20.____

21. The Daled Corporation has applied to their bank for a $50,000 loan which they will need for 90 days. The bank grants the loan, which will be discounted at 7% interest (use a 360-day year).
The Daled Corporation will receive credit in their account at the bank for

A. $46,500   B. $49,125   C. $50,000   D. $50,875

21.____

Questions 22-25.

DIRECTIONS: Questions 22 through 25 are to be answered on the basis of the information below.

Assume that you are reviewing some accounts of a company and find the following: the Machinery Account and the Accumulated Depreciation - Machinery Account.

Machinery

Jan. 1, 2014	Machine #1	20,000	July 1, 2015	6,000
Jan. 1, 2015	Machine #2	16,000		
July 1, 2015	Machine #3	12,000		
Jan. 1, 2017	Machine #4	20,000		

Accumulated Depreciation - Machinery

| | Dec. 31, 2014 | 5,000 |
| | Dec. 31, 2015 | 10,500 |

Machines are depreciated based upon a four-year life and using the straight-line method. Assume no salvage values.

On July 1, 2015 Machine #1, purchased on January 1, 2014, was sold for $6,000 cash. The bookkeeper debited Cash and credited Machinery for $6,000.

On January 1, 2017, Machine #2 was traded in for a newer model. The new machine had a list price of $34,000. A trade-in value of $10,000 was granted. $20,000 was paid in cash, and the bookkeeper debited Machinery and credited Cash for $20,000. Income tax rules should have been applied making this entry.

If any errors were made in recording the machine values or depreciation, you are asked to correct them and determine the corrected asset values and proper accumulated depreciation.

22. As of December 31, 2014, you determine that these two accounts   22._____

    A. are correct
    B. are incorrect
    C. overstate asset book values
    D. understate asset book values

23. As of December 31, 2015, you determine that to correct the Machinery Account balance   23._____
    you should leave it

    A. unchanged
    B. increased by $6,000
    C. decreased by $14,000
    D. decreased by $5,500

24. As of December 31, 2015, you determine that, to reflect the proper balance, the Accumu-   24._____
    lated Depreciation -Machinery account should

    A. remain unchanged
    B. be increased by $10,000
    C. be decreased by $10,000
    D. be decreased by $5,500

25. After the January 1, 2017 entry, you determine that the Machinery Account should prop-   25._____
    erly

    A. remain unchanged
    B. reflect a corrected balance of $52,000
    C. reflect a corrected balance of $40,000
    D. reflect a corrected balance of $56,000

Questions 26-29.

DIRECTIONS: Questions 26 through 29 are to be answered on the basis of the information below.

Assume that you are assigned to prepare an Audit Report Summary on the L Company. The L Company uses the accrual method and has an accounting year ending December 31. The bookkeeper of the company has made the following errors:

1. A $1,500 collection from a customer was received on December 29, 2016, but not recorded until the date of its deposit in the bank, January 4, 2017.
2. A supplier's $1,900 invoice for inventory items received December 2016 was not recorded until January 2017. (Inventories at December 31, 2016 and 2017 were stated correctly, based on physical count.)
3. Depreciation for 2016 was understated by $700.
4. In September 2016, a $350 invoice for office supplies was charged to the Utilities Expense account. Office supplies are expensed as purchased.
5. December 31, 2016, sales on account of $2,500 were recorded in January 2017, although the merchandise had been shipped and was not in the inventory.

Assume that no other errors have occurred and that no correcting entries have been made. Ignore all income taxes.

26. After correcting the errors reported above, the corrected Net Income for 2016 was   26.____

   A. overstated by $100
   B. understated by $800
   C. understated by $1,800
   D. neither understated nor overstated

27. Working Capital on December 31, 2016 was   27.____

   A. understated by $600
   B. understated by $2,300
   C. understated by $1,200
   D. neither understated nor overstated

28. Total Assets on December 31, 2017 were   28.____

   A. overstated by $1,100
   B. overstated by $1,800
   C. understated by $850
   D. neither understated nor overstated

29. The cash balance was   29.____

   A. correct as stated originally
   B. overstated by $1,500
   C. understated by $2,500
   D. understated by $1,500

30. Currently preferred terminology for statements to be presented limits the use of the term *reserve* to   30.____

   A. an actual liability of a known amount
   B. estimated liabilities
   C. appropriations of retained earnings
   D. valuation (contra) accounts

KEY (CORRECT ANSWERS)

1. A	11. B	21. B
2. C	12. B	22. A
3. B	13. D	23. C
4. C	14. C	24. C
5. D	15. C	25. C
6. C	16. D	26. A
7. B	17. C	27. A
8. A	18. C	28. B
9. D	19. C	29. D
10. C	20. D	30. C

TEST 2

DIRECTIONS: Each question or incomplete statement is followed by several suggested answers or completions. Select the one that BEST answers the question or completes the statement. *PRINT THE LETTER OF THE CORRECT ANSWER IN THE SPACE AT THE RIGHT.*

Questions 1-4.

DIRECTIONS: Questions 1 through 4 are to be answered on the basis of the information below.

Salary expense was listed as a total of $27,600 for the month of June 2017. Withholding taxes were determined to be $7,250 for income taxes and $1,170 for FICA taxes withheld from employees. Payroll deductions for employee pension fund contribution amounted to $2,500.

Assume the employer's FICA tax share is equal to the employees' and that the employer's share of pension costs is double that of the employees and the employer also pays a 3% Unemployment Insurance Tax based upon $20,000 of the wages paid. The employer pays $1,500 for health insurance plans.

1. The amount of cash that must be obtained to meet this net payroll to pay employees is   1._____
    A. $16,680   B. $19,180   C. $20,350   D. $27,600

2. The total payroll tax expense for this payroll period is   2._____
    A. $1,170   B. $1,760   C. $2,340   D. $2,940

3. The total liability for withholding and payroll taxes payable is   3._____
    A. $2,340   B. $7,250   C. $8,420   D. $10,190

4. The expense of the employer for pension and health care fringe benefits is   4._____
    A. $1,500   B. $2,500   C. $5,000   D. $6,500

Questions 5-6.

DIRECTIONS: Questions 5 and 6 are to be answered on the basis of the following.

The Victory Corporation provides an incentive plan whereby its president receives a bonus equal to 10% of the corporate income in excess of $150,000. The bonus is based upon income before income taxes but after calculating the bonus.

5. If the income for the calendar year 2016, before income taxes and before the bonus, were $480,000 and the effective tax rate is 40%, the amount of the bonus would be   5._____
    A. $15,000   B. $30,000   C. $33,000   D. $48,000

6. The income tax expense for calendar year 2016 would be   6._____
    A. $60,000   B. $132,000   C. $180,000   D. $192,000

Questions 7-8.

DIRECTIONS: Questions 7 and 8 are to be answered on the basis of the information below.

A contract has been awarded to the low bidder. This contractor will then commence construction of a building for the total contract price of $30,000,000. The expected cost of construction is $27,510,000. You are given the additional facts:

	2017	2018	2019
Contract Price as above	$30,000,000	$30,000,000	$30,000,000
Actual Cost to Date	9,170,000	13,755,000	27,510,000
Estimated Cost to Complete	18,340,000	13,755,000	---
Estimated Total Cost	$27,510,000	$27,510,000	$27,510,000
Estimated Total Income Billings	2,490,000		
	$9,000,000	$9,000,000	$9,000,000

7. For 2017, the income to be recognized on a percentage of completion basis would be

   A. $830,000
   B. $2,490,000
   C. $3,000,000
   D. $9,000,000

8. For 2018, the income to be recognized by the contractor on a percentage of completion basis would be

   A. $415,000   B. $424,500   C. $830,000   D. $1,245,000

9. If the city borrows the $9,000,000 to pay the first billing for the contract above at 10% interest for two years, and the second $9,000,000 at 7% interest for one year, then the interest costs related to this building are approximately

   A. $630,000
   B. $1,800,000
   C. $2,430,000
   D. $3,000,000

10. The books of the Monmouth Corporation show the following:

	2016	2015	2014
Average earnings for prior 3 years	$70,000	$75,000	$78,000
Net tangible assets	$40,000	$42,000	$50,000

   If it is expected that 15% would be normal earnings on net tangible assets, then the average excess earnings are

   A. $7,120   B. $8,333   C. $9,800   D. $10,800

Questions 11-15.

DIRECTIONS: Questions 11 through 15 are to be answered on the basis of the information below.

3 (#2)

When balance sheets are analyzed, working capital always receives close attention. Adequate working capital enables a company to carry sufficient inventories, meet current debts, take advantage of cash discounts, and extend favorable terms to customers. A company that is deficient in working capital and unable to do these things is in a poor competitive position.

Below is a Trial Balance as of June 30, 2017, in alphabetical order, of the Worth Corporation.

	DEBITS	CREDITS
Accounts Payable		$ 50,000
Accounts Receivable	$ 40,000	
Accrued Expenses Payable		10,000
Capital Stock		10,000
Cash	20,000	
Depreciation Expense	5,000	
Inventory	60,000	
Plant & Equipment (net)	30,000	
Retained Earnings		20,000
Salary Expense	35,000	
Sales		100,000
	$190,000	$190,000

11. The Worth Corporation's Working Capital, based on the data above, is

    A. $50,000   B. $55,000   C. $60,000   D. $65,000

11.____

12. Which one of the following transactions *increases* Working Capital?

    A. Collecting outstanding accounts receivable
    B. Borrowing money from the bank based upon a 90-day interest-bearing note payable
    C. Paying off a 60-day note payable to the bank
    D. Selling merchandise at a profit

12.____

13. The Worth Corporation's Current Ratio, based on the data above, is

    A. 1.7 to 1   B. 2 to 1   C. 2.5 to 1   D. 4 to 3

13.____

14. Which one of the following transactions *decreases* the Current Ratio?

    A. Collecting an accounts receivable
    B. Borrowing money from the bank giving a 90-day interest-bearing note payable
    C. Paying off a 60-day note payable to the bank
    D. Selling merchandise at a profit

14.____

15. The payment of a current liability, such as Payroll Taxes Payable, will

    A. *increase* the Current Ratio but have no effect on the Working Capital
    B. *increase* the Working Capital, but have no effect on the Current Ratio
    C. *decrease* both the Current Ratio and Working Capital
    D. *increase* both the Current Ratio and Working Capital

16. During the year 2016, the Camp Equipment Co. made sales to customers totaling $100,000 that were subject to sales taxes of $8,000. Net cash collections totaled $92,000. Discounts of $3,000 were allowed. During the year 2016, uncollectible accounts in the sum of $2,000 were written off the books.
    The net change in accounts receivable during the year 2016 was

    A. $10,500   B. $11,000   C. $13,000   D. $13,500

17. The Cable Co. received a $6,000, 8%, 60-day note dated May 1, 2016 from a customer. On May 16, 2016, the Cable Co. discounted the note at 6% at the bank. The net proceeds from the discounting of the note amounted to

    A. $5,954.40   B. $6,034.40   C. $6,064.80   D. $6,080.00

18. In reviewing the customers' accounts in the Accounts Receivable ledger for the entire year 2016, the following errors are discovered:
    1. A sale in the amount of $500 to the J. Brown Co. was erroneously posted to the K. Brown Co.
    2. A sales return of $100 from the Gale Co. was debited to their account.
    3. A check was received from a customer, M. White and Co. in payment of a sale of $500 less 2% discount. The check was entered properly in the cash receipts book but was posted to the M. White and Co. account in the amount of $490.

    The difference between the controlling account and its related accounts receivable schedule amounts to

    A. $90   B. $110   C. $190   D. $210

19. Assume that you are called upon to audit a cash fund. You find in the cash drawer postage stamps and I.O.U.'s signed by employees, totaling together $425. In preparing a financial report, the $425 should be reported as

    A. petty cash
    B. investments
    C. supplies and receivables
    D. cash

20. On December 31, 2016, before adjustment, Accounts Receivable had a debit balance of $60,000 and the Allowance for Uncollectible Accounts had a debit balance of $1,000. If credit losses are estimated at 5% of Accounts Receivable and the estimated method of reporting bad debts is used, then bad debts expense for the year 2016 would be reported as

    A. $1,000   B. $2,000   C. $3,000   D. $4,000

Questions 21-22.

DIRECTIONS: Questions 21 and 22 are to be answered on the basis of the information below.

Accrued salaries payable on $7,500 had not been recorded on December 31, 2015. Office supplies on hand of $2,500 at December 31, 2016 were erroneously treated as expense instead of inventory. Neither of these errors was discovered or corrected.

21. These two errors would cause the income for 2016 to be 21.____

    A. understated by $5,000
    B. overstated by $5,000
    C. understated by $10,000
    D. overstated by $10,000

22. The effect of these errors on the retained earnings at December 31, 2016 would be 22.____

    A. understated by $2,500
    B. overstated by $2,500
    C. understated by $5,000
    D. overstated by $5,000

Questions 23-24.

DIRECTIONS: Questions 23 and 24 are to be answered on the basis of the information below.

Arnold, Berg, and Cole operate a retail store under the trade name of ABC. Their partnership agreement provides for equally sharing profits and losses after salaries of $5,000 to Arnold, $10,000 to Berg, and $15,000 to Cole.

23. If the net income of the partnership (prior to salaries to partners) is $21,000, then Arnold's share of the profits, considering all aspects of the agreement, is determined to be 23.____

    A. $2,000   B. $3,000   C. $5,000   D. $7,000

24. The share of the profits that apply to Berg, similarly, is determined to be 24.____

    A. $2,000   B. $3,000   C. $5,000   D. $7,000

Questions 25-27.

DIRECTIONS: Questions 25 through 27 are to be answered on the basis of the following information.

The Kay Company currently uses FIFO for inventory valuation. Their records for the year ended June 30, 2017 reflect the following:

    July 1, 2016 inventory   100,000 units @ $7.50
    Purchases during year   400,000 units @ $8.00
    Sales during year   350,000 units @ $15.00
    Expenses exclusive of income taxes $1,290,000
    Cash balance on June 30, 2016 $250,000
    Income tax rate   45%

Assume the July 1, 2016 inventory will be the LIFO base inventory.

6 (#2)

25. If the company should change to the LIFO as of June 30, 2017, then their income before taxes for the year ended June 30, 2017, as compared with the income FIFO method, will be

   A. *increased* by $50,000
   B. *decreased* by $50,000
   C. *increased* by $100,000
   D. *decreased* by $100,000

25.____

26. Assuming the given tax rate (45%), the use of the LIFO method will result in an approximate tax expense for fiscal 2017 of

   A. $45,000   B. $50,000   C. $72,000   D. $94,500

26.____

27. Assuming the given tax rate (45%), the use of the LIFO inventory method, compared with the FIFO method, will result in a change in the approximate income tax expense for fiscal 2017 as follows:

   A. *increase* of $22,500
   B. *decrease* of $22,500
   C. *increase* of $45,000
   D. *decrease* of $45,000

27.____

28. An accountant in an agency, in addition to his regular duties, has been assigned to train you, a newly appointed assistant accountant. He is not giving you the training you believe you need in order to perform your duties. Accordingly, the most appropriate first step that you, an assistant accountant, should take in order to secure the needed training is to

   A. register for the appropriate courses at the local college as soon as possible
   B. advise the accountant in a formal memo that his apparent lack of interest in your training is impeding your progress
   C. discuss the matter with the accountant privately and try to discover what seems to be the problem
   D. secure such training informally from more sympathetic accountants in the agency

28.____

29. You, an assistant accountant, have worked very hard and successfully helped complete a difficult audit of a large corporation doing business in the city. Your supervisor gives you a brief nod of approval when you expected a more substantial degree of recognition. You are angry and feel unappreciated.
Of the following, the most appropriate course of action for you to take would be to

   A. voice your displeasure to your fellow workers at being taken for granted by an unappreciative supervisor
   B. say nothing now and assume that your supervisor's nod of approval may be his customary acknowledgement of efforts well done
   C. let your supervisor know that he owes you something by repeatedly stressing the outstanding job you've done
   D. ease off on your work quality and productivity until your efforts are finally appreciated

29.____

30. You, an assistant accountant, have been assisting in an audit of the books and records of businesses as a member of a team. The accountant in charge of your group tells you to start preliminary work independently on a new audit. This audit is to take place at the offices of the business. The business officers have been duly notified of the audit date. Upon arrival at their offices, you find that their records and files are in disarray and that their personnel are antagonistic and uncooperative. Of the following, the MOST desirable action for you to take is to

   A. advise the business officers that serious consequences may follow unless immediate cooperation is secured
   B. accept whatever may be shown or told you on the grounds that it would be unwise to further antagonize uncooperative personnel
   C. inform your supervisor of the situation and request instructions
   D. leave immediately and return later in the expectation of encountering a more cooperative attitude

KEY (CORRECT ANSWERS)

1. A	11. C	21. C
2. B	12. D	22. A
3. D	13. B	23. A
4. D	14. B	24. D
5. B	15. A	25. B
6. C	16. B	26. C
7. A	17. B	27. B
8. A	18. D	28. C
9. C	19. C	29. B
10. B	20. D	30. C

INTERPRETING STATISTICAL DATA GRAPHS, CHARTS AND TABLES

EXAMINATION SECTION

TEST 1

DIRECTIONS: Each question or incomplete statement is followed by several suggested answers or completions. Select the one that BEST answers the question or completes the statement. *PRINT THE LETTER OF THE CORRECT ANSWER IN THE SPACE AT THE RIGHT.*

Questions 1-10.

DIRECTIONS: Questions 1 through 10 are to be answered SOLELY on the basis of the following table showing the amounts purchased by various purchasing units during 2020.

DOLLAR VOLUME PURCHASED BY EACH PURCHASING UNIT DURING EACH QUARTER OF 2020
(FIGURES SHOWN REPRESENT THOUSANDS OF DOLLARS)

Purchasing Unit	First Quarter	Second Quarter	Third Quarter	Fourth Quarter
A	578	924	698	312
B	1,426	1,972	1,586	1,704
C	366	494	430	716
D	1,238	1,708	1,884	1,546
E	730	742	818	774
F	948	1,118	1,256	788

1. The total dollar volume purchased by all of the purchasing units during 2020 approximated MOST NEARLY
   A. $2,000,000 B. $4,000,000 C. $20,000,000 D. $40,000,000

2. During which quarter was the GREATEST total dollar amount of purchases made?
   A. First B. Second C. Third D. Fourth

3. Assume that the dollar volume purchased by Unit F during 2020 exceeded the dollar volume purchased by Unit F during 2019 by 50%.
   Then, the dollar volume purchased by Unit F during 2019 was
   A. $2,055,000 B. $2,550,000 C. $2,740,000 D. $6,165,000

4. Which one of the following purchasing units showed the sharpest DECREASE in the amount purchased during the fourth quarter as compared with the third quarter?
   A. A B. B C. D D. E

1.____

2.____

3.____

4.____

5. Comparing the dollar volume purchased in the second quarter with the dollar volume purchased in the third quarter, the decrease in the dollar volume during the third quarter was PRIMARILY due to the decrease in the dollar volume purchased by Units
   A. A and B
   B. C and D
   C. C and E
   D. C and F

6. Of the following, the unit which had the LARGEST number of dollars of increased purchases from any one quarter to the next following quarter was Unit
   A. A
   B. B
   C. C
   D. D

7. Of the following, the unit with the LARGEST dollar volume of purchases during the second half of 2020 was Unit
   A. A
   B. B
   C. D
   D. F

8. Which one of the following MOST closely approximates the percentage which Unit B's total 2020 purchases represents the total 2020 purchases of all units, including Unit B?
   A. 10%
   B. 15%
   C. 25%
   D. 45%

9. Assume that research showed that each ten thousand dollars ($10,000) of purchases by Unit D during 2020 required an average of thirteen (13) man-hours of buyers' staff time.
   On that basis, which one of the following MOST closely approximates the number of man-hours of buyers' staff time required by Unit D during 2020?
   _____ man-hours.
   A. 1,800
   B. 8,000
   C. 68,000
   D. 78,000

10. Assume that research showed that each ten thousand dollars ($10,000) of purchases by Unit C during 020 required an average of ten (10) man-hours of buyers' staff time. This research also showed that during 2020 the average man-hours of buyers' staff time per ten thousand dollars of purchases required by Unit C exceeded by 25% the average man-hours of buyers' staff time per ten thousand dollars of purchases required by Unit E.
    On that basis, which one of the following MOST closely approximates the number of buyers' staff man-hours required by Unit E during 2020?
    _____ man-hours.
    A. 2,200
    B. 2,400
    C. 3,000
    D. 3,700

KEY (CORRECT ANSWERS)

1. C
2. B
3. C
4. A
5. A
6. B
7. C
8. C
9. B
10. B

TEST 2

Questions 1-6.

DIRECTIONS: Questions 1 through 6 are to be answers SOLELY on the basis of the information contained in the five charts below. *PRINT THE LETTER OF THE CORRECT ANSWER IN THE SPACE AT THE RIGHT.*

NUMBER OF UNITS OF WORK PRODUCED IN THE BUREAU PER YEAR

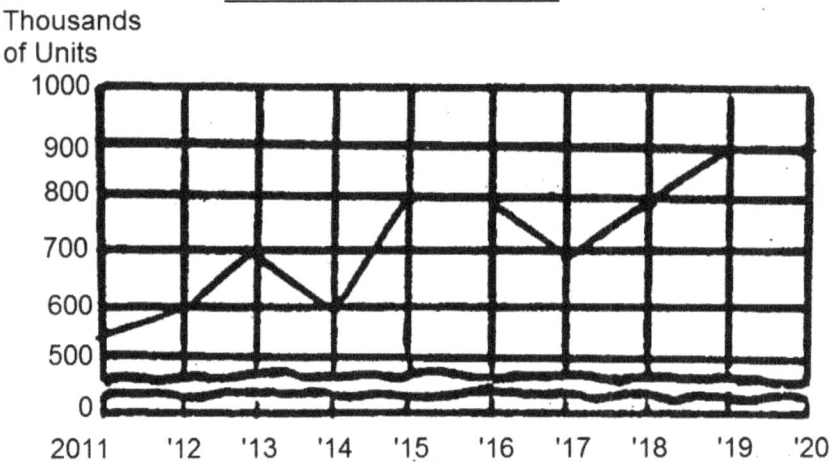

INCREASE IN THE NUMBER OF UNITS OF WORK PRODUCED IN 2020 OVER THE NUMBER PRODUCED IN 2011, BY BOROUGH

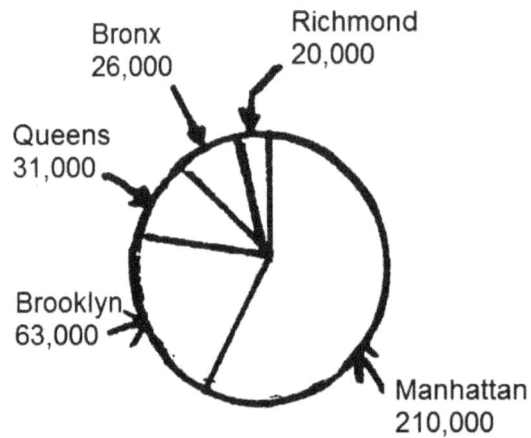

Bronx 26,000
Richmond 20,000
Queens 31,000
Brooklyn 63,000
Manhattan 210,000

NUMBER OF MALE AND FEMALE EMPLOYEES PRODUCING THE UNITS OF WORK IN THE BUREAU PER YEAR

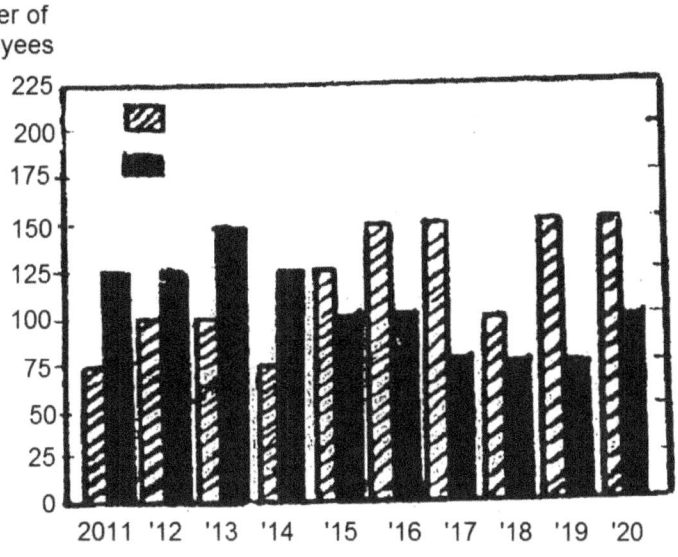

DISTRIBUTION OF THE AGES BY PERCENT OF EMPLOYEES ASSIGNED TO PRODUCE THE UNITS OF WORK IN THE YEARS 2011 AND 2020

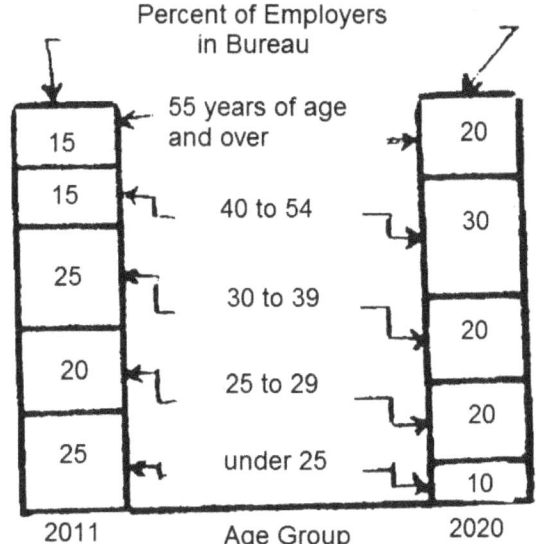

TOTAL SALARIES PAID PER YEAR TO EMPLOYEES ASSIGNED TO PRODUCE THE UNITS OF WORK IN THE BUREAU

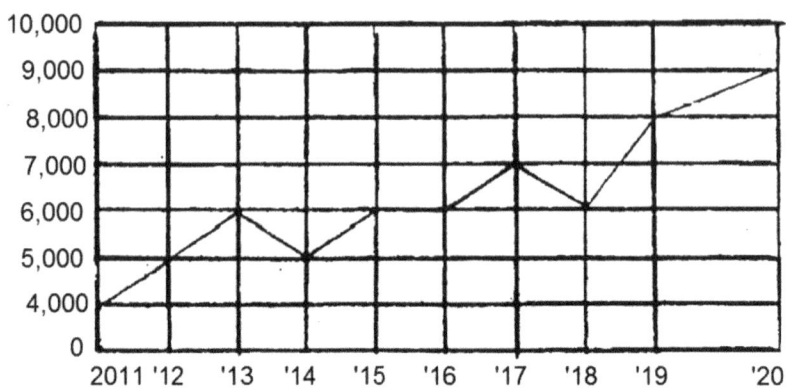

1. The information contained in the charts is sufficient to determine the
   A. amount of money paid in salaries to employees working in Richmond in 2020
   B. difference between the average annual salary of employees in the Bureau in 2020 and their average annual salary in 2019
   C. number of female employees in the Bureau between 30 and 39 years of age who were employed in 2011
   D. cost, in salary, for the average male employee in the Bureau to produce 100 units of work in 2016

2. The one of the following which was GREATER in the Bureau in 2016 than it was in 2014 was the
   A. cost, in salaries, of producing a unit of work
   B. units of work produced annually per employee
   C. proportion of female employees to total number of employees
   D. average annual salary per employee

3. If, in 2020, one-half of the employees in the Bureau 55 years of age and over each earned an annual salary of $42,000, then the average annual salary of all the remaining employees in the Bureau was MOST NEARLY
   A. $31,750   B. $34,500   C. $35,300   D. $35,800

4. Assume that, in 2011, the offices in Richmond and the Bronx each produced the same number of units of work. Also assume that, in 2011, the offices in Brooklyn, Manhattan, and Queens each produced twice as many units of work as were produced in either of the other two boroughs.
   Then, the number of units of work produced in Brooklyn in 2010 was MOST NEARLY
   A. 69,000   B. 138,000   C. 201,000   D. 225,000

5. If, in 2008, the average annual salary of the female employees in the Bureau was four-fifths as large as the average annual salary of the male employees, then the average annual salary of the female employees in that year was
   A. $37,500   B. $31,000   C. $30,500   D. $30,000

6. Of the total number of employees in the Bureau who were 30 years of age and over in 2011, _____ must have been _____.
   A. at least 35; females
   B. less than 75; males
   C. no more than 100; females
   D. more than 15; males

KEY (CORRECT ANSWERS)

1. B   4. C
2. B   5. D
3. C   6. A

TEST 3

Questions 1-10.

DIRECTIONS: Questions 1 through 10 are to be answered SOLELY on the basis of the REPORT OF TELEPHONE CALLS table given below. *PRINT THE LETTER OF THE CORRECT ANSWER IN THE SPACE AT THE RIGHT.*

	TABLE – REPORT OF TELEPHONE CALLS						
Dept.	No. of Stations	No. of Employees	No. of Incoming Calls		No. of Long Distance Calls		No. of Divisions
			2019	2020	2019	2020	
I	11	40	3421	4292	72	54	5
II	36	220	10392	10191	75	78	18
III	53	250	85243	85084	103	98	8
IV	24	60	9675	10123	82	85	6
V	13	30	5208	5492	54	48	6
VI	25	35	7472	8109	86	90	5
VII	37	195	11412	11299	68	72	11
VIII	36	54	8467	8674	59	68	4
IX	163	306	294321	289968	289	321	13
X	40	83	9588	8266	93	89	5
XI	24	68	7867	7433	86	87	13
XII	50	248	10039	10208	101	95	30
XIII	10	230	7550	6941	28	21	10
XIV	25	103	14281	14392	48	40	5
XV	19	230	8475	9206	38	43	8
XVI	22	45	4684	5584	39	48	10
XVII	41	58	10102	9677	49	52	6
XVIII	82	106	106242	105899	128	132	10
XIX	6	13	2649	2498	35	29	2
XX	16	30	1395	1468	7890	2	

1. The department which had more than 106,000 incoming calls in 2019 but fewer than 250,000 is
   A. II   B. IX   C. XVIII   D. III

   1.____

2. The department which has fewer than 8 divisions and more than 100 but fewer than 300 employees is
   A. VII   B. XIV   C. XV   D. XVIII

   2.____

3. The department which had an increase in 2020 over 2019 in the number of both incoming and long distance calls but had an increase in long distance calls of not more than 3 is
   A. IV   B. VI   C. XVII   D. XVIII

   3.____

2 (#3)

4. The department which had a decrease in the number of incoming calls in 2020 as compared to 2019 and has not less than 6 nor more than 7 divisions is
   A. IV   B. V   C. XVII   D. III

4.____

5. The department which has more than 7 divisions and more than 200 employees but fewer than 19 stations is
   A. XV   B. III   C. XX   D. XIII

5.____

6. The department having more than 10 divisions and fewer than 36 stations, which had an increase in long distance calls in 2020 over 2019 is
   A. XI   B. VII   C. XVI   D. XVIII

6.____

7. The department which in 2020 had at least 7,250 incoming calls and a decrease in long distance calls from 2019, and has more than 50 stations is
   A. IX   B. XII   C. XVIII   D. III

7.____

8. The department which has fewer than 25 stations, fewer than 100 employees, 10 or more divisions, and showed an increase of at least 9 long distance calls in 2020 over 2019 is
   A. IX   B. XVI   C. XX   D. XIII

8.____

9. The department which has more than 50 but fewer than 125 employee and had more than 5,000 incoming calls in 2019 but not more than 10,000, and more than 60 long distance calls in 2020 but not more than 85, and has more than 24 stations is
   A. VIII   B. XIV   C. IV   D. XI

9.____

10. If the number of departments showing an increase in long distance calls in 2020 over 2019 exceeds the number showing a decrease in long distance calls in the same period, select the Roman numeral indicating the department having less than one station for each 10 employees, provided not more than 8 divisions are served by that department.
    If the number of departments showing an increase in long distance calls in 2020 over 2019 does not exceed the number showing a decrease in long distance calls in the same period, select the Roman numeral indicating the department having the SMALLEST number of incoming calls in 2020.
    A. III   B. XIII   C. XV   D. XX

10.____

KEY (CORRECT ANSWERS)

1. C
2. B
3. A
4. C
5. D
6. A
7. D
8. B
9. A
10. C

TEST 4

Questions 1-7.

DIRECTIONS: Questions 1 through 7 are to be answered SOLELY on the basis of the following chart. *PRINT THE LETTER OF THE CORRECT ANSWER IN THE SPACE AT THE RIGHT.*

EMPLOYABILITY CLASSIFICATION OF PERSONS RECEIVING HOME RELIEF OR VETERANS' ASSISTANCE AT WELFARE CENTER V, JANUARY 1, THIS YEAR				
Employability Classification	Home Relief		Veterans' Assistance	
	Full	Supplementary	Full	Supplementary
Employable	369	207	15	42
Employed	330	83	2	35
Not Available for Employment	550	129	27	93
Awaiting employment conference	24	4	1	3
In rehabilitation	81	18	1	21
Attending school	26	16	3	13
In training	78	24	4	4
Temporary family care duties	32	19	6	7
Permanent family care duties	166	7	8	25
Unverified health condition	77	22	1	3
Temporary health condition	66	19	3	17
Permanently unemployable	47	8	1	37
TOTAL	1296	427	45	207

1. Of the persons on Home Relief who are either employed or employable, the percentage who are employable and are receiving full assistance is MOST NEARLY
   A. 30% B. 35% C. 50% D. 65%

   1._____

2. Assume that it is possible each month to reduce the number of Home Relief clients who are not available for employment and who are receiving full assistance by 10% from the previous month.
   By June 1, this year, the number of such Home Relief clients would be MOST NEARLY
   A. 225 B. 275 C. 325 D. 375

   2._____

3. During the month of January, this year, of the full-assistance clients on Home Relief who were not available for employment because of temporary health conditions, 42% were removed from the relief rolls, and another 26% were reassigned to supplementary Home Relief assistance because of temporary health conditions.
   Taking figures to the nearest whole number, the number of all remaining Home Relief clients, including both full and supplementary assistance at Welfare Center V is MOST NEARLY
   A. 1250 B. 1265 C. 1675 D. 1695

   3._____

2 (#4)

4. The one of the following figures which is MOST likely to require checking for accuracy or investigating for significance is the figure for persons
   A. not available for employment who are receiving supplementary Veterans' Assistance
   B. receiving full Home Relief assistance who are employed
   C. receiving supplementary Home Relief assistance who are not available for employment because they are in rehabilitation
   D. receiving supplementary Veterans' Assistance who are permanently unemployable

5. With regard to clients receiving full Veterans' Assistance, the average monthly allotment per client in the various categories is as follows: Employable $168.06; Employed $194.92; Not Available for Employment $130.74; and Permanently Unemployable $112.56.
   The average monthly allotment for all clients receiving full Veterans' Assistance at Welfare Center V is MOST NEARLY
   A. $140.06   B. $145.64   C. $151.58   D. $162.26

6. If all the Employable Home Relief clients on full assistance were to find employment so that 2/3 of them would no longer need any assistance and the rest would need only supplementary assistance, then the ratio of all Home Relief clients on full assistance to all Home Relief clients on supplementary assistance would be MOST NEARLY
   A. 2:1   B. 3:1   C. 3:2   D. 5:3

7. Assume that, for the category of Veterans' Assistance, the Federal government were to pay 2/3 of the first $60 of assistance given to each client, and 1/2 of the balance, on the basis of the average amount of assistance given to all veterans at a welfare center. Assume further that the average supplementary assistance given is $72, and the average full assistance is $140 at Welfare Center V.
   Under this plan, the amount of Veterans' Assistance given by Welfare Center V for which they would be reimbursed by the Federal government will be MOST NEARLY
   A. $8,000   B. $11,000   C. $13,000   D. $17,000

KEY (CORRECT ANSWERS)

1. B   5. B
2. C   6. D
3. D   7. C
4. B

TEST 5

Questions 1-10.

DIRECTIONS: Questions 1 through 10 are to be answered SOLELY on the basis of the Personnel Record of Division X shown below. *PRINT THE LETTER OF THE CORRECT ANSWER IN THE SPACE AT THE RIGHT.*

				DIVISION X PERSONNEL RECORD – CURRENT YEAR		
	Bureau in Which		Annual	No. of Days Absent		No. of
Employee	Employed	Title	Salary	On Vacation	On Sick Leave	Times Late
Abbott	Mail	Clerk	$31,200	18	0	1
Barnes	Mail	Clerk	$25,200	25	3	7
Davis	Mail	Typist	$24,000	21	9	2
Adams	Payroll	Accountant	$42,500	10	0	2
Bell	Payroll	Bookkeeper	$31,200	23	2	5
Duke	Payroll	Clerk	$27,600	24	4	3
Gross	Payroll	Clerk	$21,600	12	5	7
Lane	Payroll	Stenographer	$26,400	19	16	20
Reed	Payroll	Typist	$22,800	15	11	11
Arnold	Record	Clerk	$32,400	6	15	9
Cane	Record	Clerk	$24,500	14	3	4
Fay	Record	Clerk	$21,100	20	0	4
Hale	Record	Typist	$25,200	18	2	7
Baker	Supply	Clerk	$30,000	20	3	2
Clark	Supply	Clerk	$27,600	25	6	5
Ford	Supply	Typist	$22,800	25	4	22

1. The percentage of the total number of employees who are clerks is MOST NEARLY
   A. 25%   B. 33%   C. 38%   D. 56%

2. Of the following employees, the one who receives a monthly salary of $2,100 is
   A. Barnes   B. Gross   C. Reed   D. Clark

3. The difference between the annual salary of the highest paid clerk and that of the lowest paid clerk is
   A. $6,000   B. $8,400   C. $11,300   D. $20,900

4. The number of employees receiving more than $25,000 a year but less than $40,000 a year is
   A. 6   B. 9   C. 12   D. 15

5. The TOTAL annual salary of the employees of the Mail Bureau is _____ the total annual salary of the employees of the _____.
   A. one-half of; Payroll Bureau
   B. less than; Record Bureau by $21,600
   C. equal to; Supply Bureau
   D. less than; Payroll Bureau by $71,600

2 (#5)

6. The average annual salary of the employees who are not clerks is MOST NEARLY
   A. $23,700   B. $25,450   C. $26,800   D. $27,850

7. If all the employees were given a 10% increase in pay, the annual salary of Lane would then be
   A. *greater* than that of Barnes by $1,320
   B. *less* than that of Bell by $4,280
   C. *equal* to that of Clark
   D. *greater* than that of Ford by $3,600

8. Of the clerks who earned less than $30,000 a year, the one who was late the FEWEST number of times was late _____ time(s).
   A. 1   B. 2   C. 3   D. 4

9. The bureau in which the employees were late the FEWEST number of times on an average age is the _____ Bureau.
   A. Mail   B. Payroll   C. Record   D. Supply

10. The MOST accurate of the following statements is that:
    A. Reed was late more often than any other typist
    B. Bell took more time off for vacation than any other employee earning $30,000 or more annually
    C. of the typist, Ford was the one who was absent the fewest number of times
    D. three clerks took no time off because of sickness

KEY (CORRECT ANSWERS)

1.	D	6.	D
2.	A	7.	A
3.	C	8.	C
4.	B	9.	A
5.	C	10.	B

TEST 6

Questions 1-8.

DIRECTIONS: Questions 1 through 8 are to be answered SOLELY on the basis of the information contained in the chart and table shown below which relate to Bureau X in a certain public agency. The chart shows the percentage of the bureau's annual expenditures spent on equipment, supplies, and salaries for each of the years 2016-2020. The table shows the bureau's annual expenditures for each of the years 2016-2020. *PRINT THE LETTER OF THE CORRECT ANSWER IN THE SPACE AT THE RIGHT.*

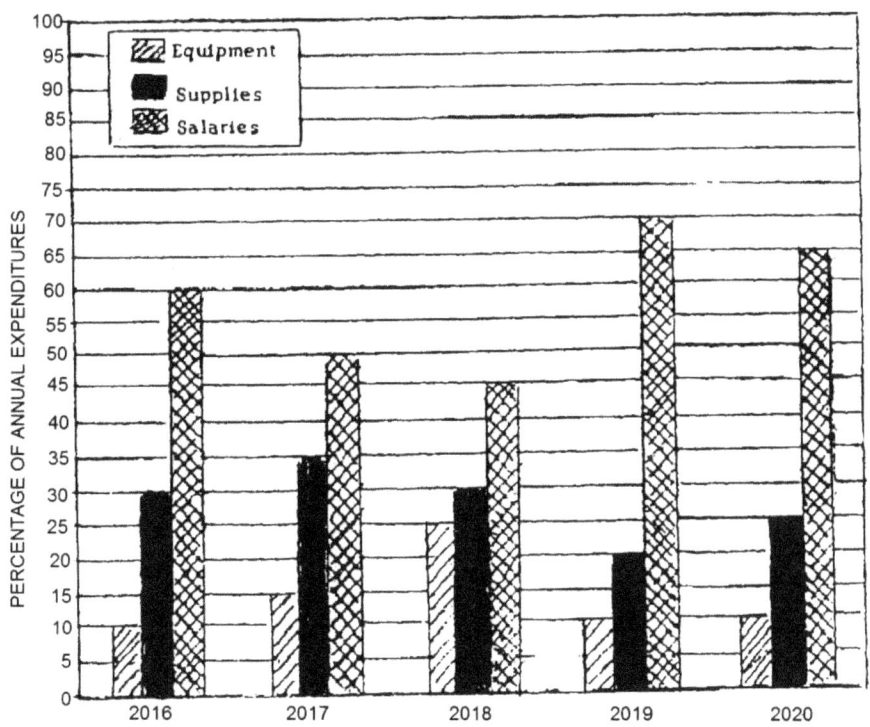

The bureau's annual expenditures for the years 2016-2020 are shown in the following table:

YEAR	EXPENDITURES
2016	$8,000,000
2017	$12,000,000
2018	$15,000,000
2019	$10,000,000
2020	$12,000,000

Equipment, supplies, and salaries were the only three categories for which the bureau spent money.

2 (#6)

Candidates may find it useful to arrange their computations on their scratch paper in an orderly manner since the correct computations for one question may also be helpful in answering another question.

1. The information contained in the chart and table is sufficient to determine the
   A. average annual salary of an employee in the bureau in 2017
   B. decrease in the amount of money spent on supplies in the bureau in 2016 from the amount spent in the preceding year
   C. changes between 2018 and 2019 in the prices of supplies bought by the bureau
   D. increase in the amount of money spent on salaries in the bureau in 2020 over the amount spent in the preceding year

2. If the percentage of expenditures for salaries in one year is added to the percentage of expenditures for equipment in that year, a total of two percentages for that year is obtained.
   The two years for which this total is the SAME are
   A. 2016 and 2018   B. 2017 and 2019
   C. 2016 and 2019   D. 2017 and 2020

3. Of the following, the year in which the bureau spent the GREATEST amount of money on supplies was
   A. 2020   B. 2018   C. 2017   D. 2016

4. Of the following years, the one in which there was the GREATEST increase over the preceding year in the amount of money spent on salaries is
   A. 2019   B. 2020   C. 2017   D. 2018

5. Of the bureau's expenditures for equipment in 2020, one-third was used for the purchase of mailroom equipment and the remainder was spent on miscellaneous office equipment.
   How much did the bureau spend on miscellaneous office equipment in 2020?
   A. $4,000,000   B. $400,000   C. $8,000,000   D. $800,000

6. If there were 120 employees in the bureau in 2019, then the average annual salary paid to the employees in that year was MOST NEARLY
   A. $43,450   B. $49,600   C. $58,350   D. $80,800

7. In 2018, the bureau had 125 employees.
   If 20 of the employees earned an average annual salary of $80,000, then the average salary of the other 105 employees was MOST NEARLY
   A. $49,000   B. $64,000   C. $41,000   D. $54,000

8. Assume that the bureau estimated that the amount of money it would spend on supplies in 2021 would be the same as the amount it spent on that category in 2020. Similarly, the bureau estimated that the amount of money it would spend on equipment in 2021 would be the same as the amount it spent on that category in 2020. However, the bureau estimated that in 2021 the amount it would spent on salaries would be 10 percent higher than the amount it spent on that category in 2020.
The percentage of its annual expenditures that the bureau estimated it would spend on supplies in 2021 is MOST NEARLY
   A. 27.5%   B. 23.5%   C. 22.5%   D. 25%

8.____

KEY (CORRECT ANSWERS)

1.	D		5.	D
2.	A		5.	C
3.	B		7.	A
4.	C		8.	B

TEST 7

Questions 1-5.

DIRECTIONS: Column I lists five kinds of statistical data which are to be transformed into a chart or a graph for incorporation into the department annual report. Column II lists nine different kinds of graphs or charts. For each type of information listed in Column I, select the chart or graph from Column II by means of which it should be demonstrated. *PRINT THE LETTER OF THE CORRECT ANSWER IN THE SPACE AT THE RIGHT.*

Column I

Column II

1. The relationship between employees' occupational classification and their salaries, for all employees by occupational classification, showing minimum, maximum, and average salary in each group.

A.

B.

1.____

2. A comparison of the number of employees in the department, the departmental budget, the number of employees in the operating divisions and the operating division budget for each year over a ten-year period.

C.

2.____

3. The amount of money spent for each of department's 10 most important functions during the past year

D.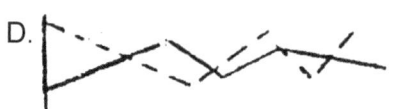

3.____

4. The percentage of the department's budget spent for each of the department's activities for each year over a ten-year period.

E.

4.____

5. The number of each kind of employee employed in the department over a period of twenty years and the total number of employees in the department for each of these periods.

F.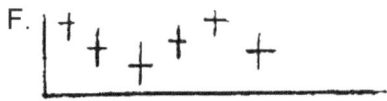

5.____

G.

H.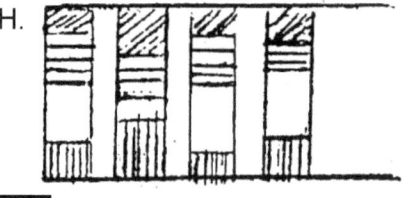

KEY (CORRECT ANSWERS)

1. F
2. D
3. C
4. H
5. G

PREPARING WRITTEN MATERIAL

PARAGRAPH REARRANGEMENT
COMMENTARY

The sentences that follow are in scrambled order. You are to rearrange them in proper order and indicate the letter choice containing the correct answer at the space at the right.

Each group of sentences in this section is actually a paragraph presented in scrambled order. Each sentence in the group has a place in that paragraph; no sentence is to be left out. You are to read each group of sentences and decide upon the best order in which to put the sentences so as to form a well-organized paragraph.

The questions in this section measure the ability to solve a problem when all the facts relevant to its solution are not given.

More specifically, certain positions of responsibility and authority require the employee to discover connection between events sometimes, apparently, unrelated. In order to do this, the employee will find it necessary to correctly infer that unspecified events have probably occurred or are likely to occur. This ability becomes especially important when action must be taken on incomplete information.

Accordingly, these questions require competitors to choose among several suggested alternatives, each of which presents a different sequential arrangement of the events. Competitors must choose the MOST logical of the suggested sequences.

In order to do so, they may be required to draw on general knowledge to infer missing concepts or events that are essential to sequencing the given events. Competitors should be careful to infer only what is essential to the sequence. The plausibility of the wrong alternatives will always require the inclusion of unlikely events or of additional chains of events which are NOT essential to sequencing the given events.

It's very important to remember that you are looking for the best of the four possible choices, and that the best choice of all may not even be one of the answers you're given to choose from.

There is no one right way to solve these problems. Many people have found it helpful to first write out the order of the sentences, as they would have arranged them, on their scrap paper before looking at the possible answers. If their optimum answer is there, this can save them some time. If it isn't, this method can still give insight into solving the problem. Others find it most helpful to just go through each of the possible choices, contrasting each as they go along. You should use whatever method feels comfortable and works for you.

While most of these types of questions are not that difficult, we've added a higher percentage of the difficult type, just to give you more practice. Usually there are only one or two questions on this section that contain such subtle distinctions that you're unable to answer confidently. And you then may find yourself stuck deciding between two possible choices, neither of which you're sure about.

EXAMINATION SECTION

TEST 1

DIRECTIONS: The following groups of sentences need to be arranged in an order that makes sense. Select the letter preceding the sequence that represents the BEST sentence order. *PRINT THE LETTER OF THE CORRECT ANSWER IN THE SPACE AT THE RIGHT.*

1. I. The keyboard was purposely designed to be a little awkward to slow typists down.
    II. The arrangement of letters on the keyboard of a typewriter was not designed for the convenience of the typist.
    III. Fortunately, no one is suggesting that a new keyboard be designed right away.
    IV. If one were, we would have to learn to type all over again.
    V. The reason was that the early machines were slower than the typists and would jam easily.
    The CORRECT answer is:
    A. I, III, IV, II, V
    B. II, V, I, IV, III
    C. V, I, II, III, IV
    D. II, I, V, III, IV

    1.____

2. I. The majority of the new service jobs are part-time or low-paying.
    II. According to the U.S. Bureau of Labor Statistics, jobs in the service sector constitute 72% of all jobs in this country.
    III. If more and more workers receive less and less money, who will buy the goods and services needed to keep the economy going?
    IV. The service sector is by far the fastest growing part of the United States economy.
    V. Some economists look upon this trend with great concern.
    The CORRECT answer is:
    A. II, IV, I, V, III
    B. II, III, IV, I, V
    C. V, IV, II, III, I
    D. III, I, II, IV, V

    2.____

3. I. They can also affect one's endurance.
    II. This can stabilize blood sugar levels, and ensure that the brain is receiving a steady, constant, supply of glucose, so that one is *hitting on all cylinders* while taking the test.
    III. By food, we mean real food, not junk food or unhealthy snacks.
    IV. For this reason, it is important not to skip a meal, and to bring food with you to the exam.
    V. One's blood sugar levels can affect how clearly one is able to think and concentrate during an exam.
    The CORRECT answer is:
    A. V, IV, II, III, I
    B. V, II, I, IV, III
    C. V, I, IV, III, II
    D. V, IV, I, III, II

    3.____

4.
  I. Those who are the embodiment of desire are absorbed in material quests, and those who are the embodiment of feeling are warriors who value power more than possession.
  II. These qualities are in everyone, but in different degrees.
  III. But those who value understanding yearn not for goods or victory, but for knowledge.
  IV. According to Plato, human behavior flows from three main sources: desire, emotion, and knowledge.
  V. In the perfect state, the industrial forces would produce but not rule, the military would protect but not rule, and the forces of knowledge, the philosopher kings, would reign.
  The CORRECT answer is:
  A. IV, V, I, II, III
  B. V, I, II, III, IV
  C. IV, III, II, I, V
  D. IV, II, I, III, V

4.____

5.
  I. Of the more than 26,000 tons of garbage produced daily in New York City, 12,000 tons arrive daily at Fresh Kills.
  II. In a month, enough garbage accumulates there to fill the Empire State Building.
  III. In 1937, the Supreme Court halted the practice of dumping the trash of New York City into the sea.
  IV. Although the garbage is compacted, in a few years the mounds of garbage at Fresh Kills will be the highest points south of Maine's Mount Desert Island on the Eastern Seaboard.
  V. Instead, tugboats now pull barges of much of the trash to Staten Island and the largest landfill in the world, Fresh Kills.
  The CORRECT answer is:
  A. III, V, IV, I, II
  B. III, V, II, IV, I
  C. III, V, I, II, IV
  D. III, II, V, IV, I

5.____

6.
  I. Communists rank equality very high, but freedom very low.
  II. Unlike communists, conservatives place a high value on freedom and a very low value on equality.
  III. A recent study demonstrated that one way to classify people's political beliefs is to look at the importance placed on two words: freedom and equality.
  IV. Thus, by demonstrating how members of these groups feel about the two words, the study has proved to be useful for political analysts in several European countries.
  V. According to the study, socialists and liberals rank both freedom and equality very high, while fascists rate both very low.
  The CORRECT answer is:
  A. III, V, I, II, IV
  B. V, IV, III, I, II
  C. III, V, IV, II, I
  D. III, I, II, IV, V

6.____

7. I. "Can there be anything more amazing than this?"
    II. If the riddle is successfully answered, his dead brothers will be brought back to life.
    III. "Even though man sees those around him dying every day," says Dharmaraj, "he still believes and acts as if he were immortal."
    IV. "What is the cause of ceaseless wonder?" asks the Lord of the Lake.
    V. In the ancient epic, <u>The Mahabharata</u>, a riddle is asked of one of the Pandava brothers.
    The CORRECT answer is:
    A. V, II, I, IV, III
    B. V, IV, III, I, II
    C. V, II, IV, III, I
    D. V, II, IV, I, III

7.____

8. I. On the contrary, the two main theories—the cooperative (neoclassical) theory and the radical (labor theory)—clearly rest on very different assumptions, which have very different ethical overtones.
    II. The distribution of income is the primary factor in determining the relative levels of material well-being that different groups or individuals attain.
    III. Of all issues in economics, the distribution of income is one of the most controversial.
    IV. The neoclassical theory tends to support the existing income distribution (or minor changes), while the labor theory ends to support substantial changes in the way income is distributed.
    V. The intensity of the controversy reflects the fact that different economic theories are not purely neutral, *detached* theories with no ethical or moral implications.
    The CORRECT answer is:
    A. II, I, V, IV, III
    B. III, II, V, I, IV
    C. III, V, II, I, IV
    D. III, V, IV, I, II

8.____

9. I. The pool acts as a broker and ensures that the cheapest power gets used first.
    II. Every six seconds, the pool's computer monitors all of the generating stations in the state and decides which to ask for more power and which to cut back.
    III. The buying and selling of electrical power is handled by the New York Power Pool in Guilderland, New York.
    IV. This is to the advantage of both the buying and selling utilities.
    V. The pool began operation in 1970, and consists of the state's eight electric utilities.
    The CORRECT answer is:
    A. V, I, II, III, IV
    B. IV, II, I, III, V
    C. III, V, I, IV, II
    D. V, III, IV, II, I

9.____

10. I. Modern English is much simpler grammatically than Old English.
    II. Finnish grammar is very complicated; there are some fifteen cases, for example.
    III. Chinese, a very old language, may seem to be the exception, but it is the great number of characters/words that must be mastered that makes it so difficult to learn, not its grammar.
    IV. The newest literary language—that is, written as well as spoken—is Finish, whose literary roots go back only to about the middle of the nineteenth century.
    V. Contrary to popular belief, the longer a language is been in use the simpler its grammar—not the reverse.
    The CORRECT answer is:
    A. IV, I, II, III, V
    B. V, I, IV, II, III
    C. I, II, IV, III, V
    D. IV, II, III, I, V

KEY (CORRECT ANSWERS)

1.	D	6.	A
2.	A	7.	C
3.	C	8.	B
4.	D	9.	C
5.	C	10.	B

TEST 2

DIRECTIONS: This type of question tests your ability to recognize accurate paraphrasing, well-constructed paragraphs, and appropriate style and tone. It is important that the answer you select contains only the facts or concepts given in the original sentences. It is also important that you be aware of incomplete sentences, inappropriate transitions, unsupported opinions, incorrect usage, and illogical sentence order. Paragraphs that do not include all the necessary facts and concepts, that distort them, or that add new ones are not considered correct.

The format for this section may vary. Sometimes, long paragraphs are given, and emphasis is placed on style and organization. Our first five questions are of this type. Other times, the paragraphs are shorter, and there is less emphasis on style and more emphasis on accurate representation of information. Our second group of five questions are of this nature.

For each of Questions 1 through 10, select the paragraph that BEST expresses the ideas contained in the sentences above it. *PRINT THE LETTER OF THE CORRECT ANSWER IN THE SPACE AT THE RIGHT.*

1.
   I. Listening skills are very important for managers.
   II. Listening skills are not usually emphasized.
   III. Whenever managers are depicted in books, manuals or the media, they are always talking, never listening.
   IV. We'd like you to read the enclosed handout on listening skills and to try to consciously apply them this week.
   V. We guarantee they will improve the quality of your interactions.

   1.____

   A. Unfortunately, listening skills are not usually emphasized for managers. Managers are always depicted as talking, never listening. We'd like you to read the enclosed handout on listening skills. Please try to apply these principles this week. If you do, we guarantee they will improve the quality of your interactions.
   B. The enclosed handout on listening skills will be important improving the quality of your interactions. We guarantee it. All you have to do is take sometime this week to read and to consciously try to apply the principles. Listening skills are very important for manages, but they are not usually emphasized. Whenever managers are depicted in books, manuals or the media, they are always talking, never listening.
   C. Listening well is one of the most important skills a manager can have, yet it's not usually given much attention. Think about any representation of managers in books, manuals, or in the media that you may have seen. They're always talking, never listening. We'd like you to read the enclosed handout on listening skills and consciously try to apply them the rest of the week. We guarantee you will see a difference in the quality of your interactions.

D. Effective listening, one very important tool in the effective manager's arsenal, is usually not emphasized enough. The usual depiction of managers in books, manuals or the media is one in which they are always talking, never listening. We'd like you to read the enclosed handout and consciously try to apply the information contained therein throughout the rest of the week. We feel sure that you will see a marked difference in the quality of your interactions.

2. I. Chekhov wrote three dramatic masterpieces which share certain themes and formats: Uncle Vanya, The Cherry Orchard, and The Three Sisters.
    II. They are primarily concerned with the passage of time and how this erodes human aspirations.
    III. The plays are haunted by the ghosts of the wasted life.
    IV. The characters are concerned with life's lesser problems; however, such as the inability to make decisions, loyalty to the wrong cause, and the inability to be clear.
    V. This results in sweet, almost aching, type of a sadness referred to as Chekhovian.

    2._____

    A. Chekhov wrote three dramatic masterpieces: Uncle Vanya, The Cherry Orchard, and The Three Sisters. These masterpieces share certain themes and formats: the passage of time, how time erodes human aspirations, and the ghosts of wasted life. Each masterpiece is characterized by a sweet, almost aching, type of sadness that has become known as Chekhovian. The sweetness of this sadness hinges on the fact that it is not the great tragedies of life which are destroying these characters, but their minor flaws: indecisiveness, misplaced loyalty, unclarity.
    B. The Cherry Orchard, Uncle Vanya, and The Three Sisters are three dramatic masterpieces written by Chekhov that use similar formats to explore a common theme. Each is primarily concerned with the way that passing time wears down human aspirations, and each is haunted by the ghosts of the wasted life. The characters are shown struggling futilely with the lesser problems of life: indecisiveness, loyalty to the wrong cause, and the inability to be clear. These struggles create a mood of sweet, almost aching, sadness that has become known as Chekhovian.
    C. Chekhov's dramatic masterpieces are, along with The Cherry Orchard, Uncle Vanya, and The Three Sisters. These plays share certain thematic and formal similarities. They are concerned most of all with the passage of time and the way in which time erodes human aspirations. Each play is haunted by the specter of the wasted life. Chekhov's characters are caught, however, by life's lesser snares: indecisiveness, loyalty to the wrong cause, and unclarity. The characteristic mood is a sweet, almost aching type of sadness that has come to be known as Chekhovian.
    D. A Chekhovian mood is characterized by sweet, almost aching, sadness. The term comes from three dramatic tragedies by Chekhov which revolve around the sadness of a wasted life. The three masterpieces (Uncle Vanya, The Three Sisters, and The Cherry Orchard) share the same

theme and format. The plays are concerned with how the passage of time erodes human aspirations. They are peopled with characters who are struggling with life's lesser problems. These are people who are indecisive, loyal to the wrong causes, or are unable to make themselves clear.

3.
I. Movie previews have often helped producers decide which parts of movies they should take out or leave in.
II. The first 1933 preview of King Kong was very helpful to the producers because many people ran screaming from the theater and would not return when four men first attacked by Kong were eaten by giant spiders.
III. The 1950 premiere of Sunset Boulevard resulted in the filming of an entirely new beginning, and a delay of six months in the film's release.
IV. In the original opening scene, William Holden was in a morgue talking with thirty-six other "corpses" about the ways some of them had died.
V. When he began to tell them of his life with Gloria Swanson, the audience found this hilarious, instead of taking the scene seriously.

3._____

A. Movie previews have often helped producers decide what parts of movies they should leave in or take out. For example, the first preview of King Kong in 1933 was very helpful. In one scene, four men were first attacked by Kong and then eaten by giant spiders. Many members of the audience ran screaming from the theater and would not return. The premiere of the 1950 film Sunset Boulevard was also very helpful. In the original opening scene, William Holden was in a morgue with thirty-six other "corpses," discussing the ways some of them had died. When he began to tell them of his life with Gloria Swanson, the audience found this hilarious. They were supposed to take the scene seriously. The result was a delay of six months in the release of the film while a new beginning was added.

B. Movie previews have often helped producers decide whether they should change various parts of a movie. After the 1933 preview of King Kong, a scene in which four men who had been attacked by Kong were eaten by giant spiders was taken out as many people ran screaming from the theater and would not return. The 1950 premiere of Sunset Boulevard also led to some changes. In the original opening scene, William Holden was in a morgue talking with thirty-six other "corpses" about the ways some of them had died. When he began to tell them of his life with Gloria Swanson, the audience found this hilarious, instead of taking the scene seriously.

C. What do Sunset Boulevard and King Kong have in common? Both show the value of using movie previews to test audience reaction. The first 1933 preview of King Kong showed that a scene showing four men being eaten by giant spiders after having been attacked by Kong was too frightening for many people. They ran screaming from the theater and couldn't be coaxed back. The 1950 premiere of Sunset Boulevard was also a scream, but not the kind the producers intended. The movie opens with William Holden lying in a morgue discussing the ways they had died with thirty-six other "corpses." When he began to tell them of his life with Gloria Swanson, the audience couldn't take him seriously. Their laughter caused a six-month delay while the beginning was rewritten.

D. Producers very often use movie previews to decide if changes are needed. The premiere of Sunset Boulevard in 1950 led to a new beginning and a six-month delay in film release. At the beginning, William Holden and thirty-six other "corpses" discuss the ways some of them died. Rather than taking this seriously, the audience thought it was hilarious when he began to tell them of his life with Gloria Swanson. The first 1933 preview of King Kong was very helpful for its producers because one scene so terrified the audience that many of them ran screaming from the theater and would not return. In this particular scene, four men who had first been attacked by Kong were eaten by giant spiders.

4.
I. It is common for supervisors to view employees as "things" to be manipulated.
II. This approach does not motivate employees, nor does the carrot-and-stick approach because employees often recognize these behaviors and resent them.
III. Supervisors can change these behaviors by using self-inquiry and persistence.
IV. The best managers genuinely respect those they work with, are supportive and helpful, and are interested in working as a team with those they supervise.
V. They disagree with the Golden Rule that says "he or she who has the gold makes the rules."

4.____

   A. Some managers act as if they think the Golden Rule means "he or she who has the gold makes the rules." They show disrespect to employees by seeing them as "things" to be manipulated. Obviously, this approach does not motivate employees any more than the carrot-and-stick approach motivates them. The employees are smart enough to spot these behaviors and resent them. On the other hand, the managers genuinely respect those they work with, are supportive and helpful, and are interested in working as a team. Self-inquiry and persistence can change even the former type of supervisor into the latter.

   B. Many supervisors all into the trap of viewing employees as "things" to be manipulated, or try to motivate them by using a carrot-and-stick approach. These methods do not motivate employees, who often recognize the behaviors and resent them. Supervisors can change these behaviors, however, by using self-inquiry and persistence. The best managers are supportive and helpful, and have genuine respect for those with whom they work. They are interested in working as a team with those they supervise. To them, the Golden Rule is not "he or she who has the gold makes the rules."

   C. Some supervisors see employees as "things" to be used or manipulated using a carrot-and-stick technique. These methods don't work. Employees often see through them and resent them. A supervisor who wants to change may do so. The techniques of self-inquiry and persistence can be used to turn him or her into the type of supervisor who doesn't think the Golden Rule is "he or she who has the gold makes the rules." They may become like the best managers who treat those with whom they work with respect and give them help and support. These are the manager who know how to build a team.

D. Unfortunately, many supervisors act as if their employees are objects whose movements they can position at will. This mistaken belief has the same result as another popular motivational technique—the carrot-and-stick approach. Both attitudes can lead to the same result—resentment from those employees who recognize the behaviors for what they are. Supervisors who recognize these behaviors can change through the use of persistence and the use of self-inquiry. It's important to remember that the best managers respect their employees. They readily give necessary help and support and are interested in working as a team with those they supervise. To these managers, the Golden Rule is not "he or she who has the gold makes the rules."

5. I. The first half of the nineteenth century produced a group of pessimistic poets—Byron, De Musset, Heine, Pushkin, and Leopardi.
   II. It also produced a group of pessimistic composers—Schubert, Chopin, Schumann, and even the later Beethoven.
   III. Above all, in philosophy, there was the profoundly pessimistic philosopher, Schopenhauer.
   IV. The Revolution was dead, the Bourbons were restored, the feudal barons were reclaiming their land, and progress everywhere was being suppressed, as the great age was over.
   V. "I thank God," said Goethe, "that I am not young in so thoroughly finished a world."

5._____

   A. "I thank God," said Goethe, "that I am not young in so thoroughly finished a world." The Revolution was dead, the Bourbons were restored, the feudal barons were reclaiming their land, and progress everywhere was being suppressed. The first half of the nineteenth century produced a group of pessimistic poets: Byron, De Musset, Heine, Pushkin, and Leopardi. It also produced pessimistic composers: Schubert, Chopin, Schumann. Although Beethoven came later, he fits into this group, too. Finally and above all, it also produced a profoundly pessimistic philosopher, Schopenhauer. The great age was over.
   B. The first half of the nineteenth century produced a group of pessimistic poets: Byron, De Musset, Heine, Pushkin, and Leopardi. It produced a group of pessimistic composers: Schubert, Chopin, Schumann, and even the later Beethoven. Above all, it produced a profoundly pessimistic philosopher, Schopenhauer. For each of these men, the great age was over. The Revolution was dead, and the Bourbons were restored. The feudal barons were reclaiming their land, and progress everywhere was being suppressed.

C. The great age was over. The Revolution was dead—the Bourbons were restored, and the feudal barons were reclaiming their land. Progress everywhere was being suppressed. Out of this climate came a profound pessimism. Poets, like Byron, De Musset, Heine, Pushkin, and Leopardi; composers, like Schubert, Chopin, Schumann, and even the later Beethoven; and above all, a profoundly pessimistic philosopher, Schopenauer. This pessimism which arose in the first half of the nineteenth century is illustrated by these words of Goethe, "I thank God that I am not young in so thoroughly finished a world."

D. The first half of the nineteenth century produced a group of pessimistic poets, Byron, De Musset, Heine, Pushkin, and Leopardi—and a group of pessimistic composers, Schubert, Chopin, Schumann, and the later Beethoven. Above it all, it produced a profoundly pessimistic philosopher, Schopenhauer. The great age was over. The Revolution was dead, the Bourbons were restored, the feudal barons were reclaiming their land, and progress everywhere was being suppressed. "I thank God," said Goethe, "that I am not young in so thoroughly finished a world."

6. I. A new manager sometimes may feel insecure about his or her competence in the new position.
   II. The new manager may then exhibit defensive or arrogant behavior towards those one supervises, or the new manager may direct overly flattering behavior toward one's new supervisor.

   A. Sometimes, a new manager may feel insecure about his or her ability to perform well in this new position. The insecurity may lead him or her to treat others differently. He or she may display arrogant or defensive behavior towards those he or she supervises, or be overly flattering to his or her new supervisor.
   B. A new manager may sometimes feel insecure about his or her ability to perform well in the new position. He or she may then become arrogant, defensive, or overly flattering towards those he or she works with.
   C. There are times when a new manager may be insecure about how well he or she can perform in the new job. The new manager may also behave defensive or act in an arrogant way towards those he or she supervises, or overly flatter his or her boss.
   D. Sometimes a new manager may feel insecure about his or her ability to perform well in the new position. He or she may then display arrogant or defensive behavior towards those they supervise, or become overly flattering towards their supervisors.

6._____

7. I. It is possible to eliminate unwanted behavior by bringing it under stimulus control—tying the behavior to a cue, and then never, or rarely, giving the cue.
   II. One trainer successfully used this method to keep an energetic young porpoise from coming out of her tank whenever she felt like it, which was potentially dangerous.
   III. Her trainer taught her to do it for a reward, in response to a hand signal, and then rarely gave the signal.

7._____

A. Unwanted behavior can be eliminated by tying the behavior to a cue, and then never, or rarely, giving the cue. This is called stimulus control. One trainer was able to use this method to keep an energetic young porpoise from coming out of her tank by teaching her to come out for a reward in response to a hand signal, and then rarely giving the signal.
B. Stimulus control can be used to eliminate unwanted behavior. In this method, behavior is tied to a cue, and then the cue is rarely, if ever, given. One trainer was able to successfully use stimulus control to keep an energetic young porpoise from coming out of her tank whenever she felt like it—a potentially dangerous practice. She taught the porpoise to come out for a reward when she gave a hand signal, and then rarely gave the signal.
C. It is possible to eliminate behavior that is undesirable by bringing it under stimulus control by tying behavior to a signal, and then rarely giving the signal. One trainer successfully used this method to keep an energetic porpoise from coming out of her tank, a potentially dangerous situation. Her trainer taught the porpoise to do it for a reward, in response to a hand signal, and then would rarely give the signal.
D. By using stimulus control, it is possible to eliminate unwanted behavior by tying the behavior to a cue, and then rarely or never give the cue. One trainer was able to use this method to successfully stop a young porpoise from coming out of her tank whenever she felt like it. To curb this potentially dangerous practice, the porpoise was taught by the trainer to come out of the tank for a reward, in response to a hand signal, and then rarely given the signal.

8. I. There is a great deal of concern over the safety of commercial trucks, caused by their greatly increased role in serious accidents since federal deregulation in 1981.
    II. Recently, 60 percent of trucks in New York and Connecticut and 70 percent of trucks in Maryland randomly stopped by state troopers failed safety inspections.
    III. Sixteen states in the United States require no training at all for truck drivers.

    8._____

    A. Since federal deregulation in 1981, there has been a great deal of concern over the safety of commercial trucks, and their greatly increased role in serious accidents. Recently, 60 percent of trucks in New York and Connecticut, and 70 percent of trucks in Maryland failed safety inspections. Sixteen states in the United States require no training at all for truck drivers.
    B. There is a great deal of concern over the safety of commercial trucks since federal deregulation in 1981. Their role in serious accidents has greatly increased. Recently, 60 percent of trucks randomly stopped in Connecticut and New York and 70 percent in Maryland failed safety inspections conducted by state troopers. Sixteen states in the United States provide no training at all for truck drivers.
    C. Commercial trucks have a greatly increased role in serious accidents since federal deregulation in 1981. This has led to a great deal of concern.

Recently, 70 percent of trucks in Maryland and 60 percent of trucks in New York and Connecticut failed inspection of those that were randomly stopped by state troopers. Sixteen states in the United States require no training for all truck drivers.

D. Since federal deregulation in 1981, the role that commercial trucks have played in serious accidents has greatly increased, and this has led to a great deal of concern. Recently, 60 percent of trucks in New York and Connecticut, and 70 percent of trucks in Maryland randomly stopped by state troopers failed safety inspections. Sixteen states in the U.S. don't require any training for truck drivers.

9.
I. No matter how much some people have, they still feel unsatisfied and want more, or want to keep what they have forever.
II. One recent television documentary showed several people flying from New York to Paris for a one-day shopping spree to buy platinum earrings, because they were bored.
III. In Brazil, some people were ordering coffins that cost a minimum of $45,000 and are equipping them with deluxe stereos, televisions, and other graveyard necessities.

9.____

A. Some people, despite having a great deal, still feel unsatisfied and want more, or think they can keep what they have forever. One recent documentary on television showed several people enroute from Paris to New York for a one day shopping spree to buy platinum earrings, because they were bored. Some people in Brazil are even ordering coffins equipped with such graveyard necessities as deluxe stereos and televisions. The price of the coffins start at $45,000.
B. No matter how much some people have, they may feel unsatisfied. This leads them to want more, or to want to keep what they have forever. Recently, a television documentary depicting several people flying from New York to Paris for a one day shopping spree to buy platinum earrings. They were bored. Some people in Brazil are ordering coffins that cost at least $45,000 and come equipped with deluxe televisions, stereos and other necessary graveyard items.
C. Some people will be dissatisfied no matter how much they have. They may want more, or they may want to keep what they have forever. One recent television documentary showed several people, motivated by boredom, jetting from New York to Paris for a one-day shopping spree to buy platinum earrings. In Brazil, some people are ordering coffins equipped with deluxe stereos, televisions and other graveyard necessities. The minimum price for these coffins—$45,000.
D. Some people are never satisfied. No matter how much they have they still want more, or think they can keep what they have forever. One television documentary recently showed several people flying from New York to Paris for the day to buy platinum earrings because they were bored. In Brazil, some people are ordering coffins that cost $45,000 and are equipped with deluxe stereos, televisions and other graveyard necessities.

10.
I. A television signal or video signal has three parts.
II. Its parts are the black-and-white portion, the color portion, and the synchronizing (sync) pulses, which keep the picture stable.
III. Each video source, whether it's a camera or a video-cassette recorder contains its own generator of these synchronizing pulses to accompany the picture that it's sending in order to keep it steady and straight.
IV. In order to produce a clean recording, a video-cassette recorder must "lock-up" to the sync pulses that are part of the video it is trying to record, and this effort may be very noticeable if the device does not have gunlock.

10._____

A. There are three parts to a television or video signal: the black-and-white part, the color part, and the synchronizing (sync) pulses, which keep the picture stable. Whether it's a video-cassette recorder or a camera, each video source contains its own pulse that synchronizes and generates the picture it's sending in order to keep it straight and steady. A video-cassette recorder must "lock up" to the sync pulses that are part of the video it's trying to record. If the device doesn't have gunlock, this effort must be very noticeable.

B. A video signal or television is comprised of three parts: the black-and-white portion, the color portion, and the sync (synchronizing) pulses, which keep the picture stable. Whether it's a camera or a video-cassette recorder, each video source contains its own generator of these synchronizing pulses. These accompany the picture that it's sending in order to keep it straight and steady. A video-cassette recorder must "lock up" to the sync pulses that are part of the video it is trying to record in order to produce a clean recording. This effort may be very noticeable if the device does not have gunlock.

C. There are three parts to a television or video signal: the color portion, the black-and-white portion, and the sync (synchronizing pulses). These keep the picture stable. Each video source, whether it's a video-cassette recorder or a camera, generates these synchronizing pulses accompanying the picture it's sending in order to keep it straight and steady. If a clean recording is to be produced, a video-cassette recorder must store the sync pulses that are part of the video it is trying to record. This effort may not be noticeable if the device does not have gunlock.

D. A television signal or video signal has three parts: the black-and-white portion, the color portion, and the synchronizing (sync) pulses. It's the sync pulses which keep the picture stable, which accompany it and keep it steady and straight. Whether it's a camera or a video-cassette recorder, each video source contains its own generator of these synchronizing pulses. To produce a clean recording, a video-cassette recorder must "lock up" to the sync pulses that are part of the video it is trying to record. If the device does not have gunlock, this effort may be very noticeable.

KEY (CORRECT ANSWERS)

1. C
2. B
3. A
4. B
5. D

6. A
7. B
8. D
9. C
10. D

PREPARING WRITTEN MATERIALS
EXAMINATION SECTION
TEST 1

DIRECTIONS: Each question or incomplete statement is followed by several suggested answers or completions. Select the one that BEST answers the question or completes the statement. *PRINT THE LETTER OF THE CORRECT ANSWER IN THE SPACE AT THE RIGHT.*

Questions 1-25.

DIRECTIONS: Questions 1 through 25 consist of sentences which may or may not be examples of good English usage. Consider grammar, punctuation, spelling, capitalization, awkwardness, etc. Examine each sentence and then choose the correct statement about it from the four choices below it. If the English usage in the sentence given is better than it would be with any of the changes suggested in options B, C, and D, choose option A. Do not choose an option that will change the meaning of the sentence.

1. According to Judge Frank, the grocer's sons found guilty of assault and sentenced last Thursday.
    A. This is an example of acceptable writing.
    B. A comma should be placed after the word *sentenced*.
    C. The word *were* should be placed after *sons*.
    D. The apostrophe in *grocer's* should be placed after the *s*.

1._____

2. The department heads assistant said that the stenographers should type duplicate copies of all contracts, leases, and bills.
    A. This is an example of acceptable writing,
    B. A comma should be placed before the word "*contracts*.
    C. An apostrophe should be placed before the *s* in *heads*.
    D. Quotation marks should be placed before the *stenographers* and after *bills*.

2._____

3. The lawyers questioned the men to determine who was the true property owner?
    A. This is an example of acceptable writing.
    B. The phrase *questioned the men* should be changed to *asked the men questions*.
    C. The word *was* should be changed to *were*.
    D. The question mark should be changed to a period.

3._____

4. The terms stated in the present contract are more specific than those stated in the previous contract.
    A. This is an example of acceptable writing,
    B. The word *are* should be changed to *is*.
    C. The word *than* should be changed to *then*.
    D. The word *specific* should be changed to *specified*.

    4.____

5. Of the few lawyers considered, the one who argued more skillful was chosen for the job.
    A. This is an example of acceptable writing.
    B. The word *more* should be replaced by the word *most*.
    C. The word *skillful* should be replaced by the word *skillfully*.
    D. The word *chosen* should be replaced by the word *selected*.

    5.____

6. Each of the states has a court of appeals; some states have circuit courts.
    A. This is an example of acceptable writing
    B. The semi-colon should be changed to a comma.
    C. The word *has* should be changed to *have*.
    D. The word *some* should be capitalized.

    6.____

7. The court trial has greatly effected the child's mental condition.
    A. This is an example of acceptable writing.
    B. The word *effected* should be changed to *affected*.
    C. The word *greatly* should be placed after *effected*.
    D. The apostrophe in *child's* should be placed after the *s*.

    7.____

8. Last week, the petition signed by all the officers was sent to the Better Business Bureau.
    A. This is an example of acceptable writing.
    B. The phrase *last week* should be placed after *officers*.
    C. A comma should be placed after *petition*.
    D. The word *was* should be changed to *were*.

    8.____

9. Mr. Farrell claims that he requested form A-12, and three booklets describing court procedures.
    A. This is an example of acceptable writing.
    B. The word *that* should be eliminated.
    C. A colon should be placed after *requested*.
    D. The comma after *A-12* should be eliminated.

    9.____

10. We attended a staff conference on Wednesday the new safety and fire rules were discussed.
    A. This is an example of acceptable writing.
    B. The words *safety*, *fire*, and *rules* should begin with capital letters.
    C. There should be a comma after the word *Wednesday*.
    D. There should be a period after the word *Wednesday*, and the word *the* should begin with a capital letter.

    10.____

11. Neither the dictionary or the telephone directory could be found in the office library.
    A. This is an example of acceptable writing.
    B. The word *or* should be changed to *nor*.
    C. The word *library* should be spelled *libery*.
    D. The word *neither* should be changed to *either*.

    11._____

12. The report would have been typed correctly if the typist could read the draft.
    A. This is an example of acceptable writing.
    B. The word *would* should be removed.
    C. The word *have* should be inserted after the word *could*.
    D. The word *correctly* should be changed to *correct*.

    12._____

13. The supervisor brought the reports and forms to an employees desk.
    A. This is an example of acceptable writing.
    B. The word *brought* should be changed to *took*.
    C. There should be a comma after the word *reports* and a comma after the word *forms*.
    D. The word *employees* should be spelled *employee's*.

    13._____

14. It's important for all the office personnel to submit their vacation schedules on time.
    A. This is an example of acceptable writing.
    B. The word *It's* should be spelled *Its*.
    C. The word *their* should be spelled *they're*.
    D. The word *personnel* should be spelled *personal*.

    14._____

15. The supervisor wants that all staff members report to the office at 9:00 A.M.
    A. This is an example of acceptable writing.
    B. The word *that* should be removed and the word *to* should be inserted after the word *members*.
    C. There should be a comma after the word *wants* and a comma after the word *office*.
    D. The word *wants* should be changed to *want* and the word *shall* should be inserted after the word *members*.

    15._____

16. Every morning the clerk opens the office mail and distributes it.
    A. This is an example of acceptable writing.
    B. The word *opens* should be changed to *letters*.
    C. The word *mail* should be changed to *letters*.
    D. The word *it* should be changed to *them*.

    16._____

17. The secretary typed more fast on a desktop computer than on a tablet.
    A. This is an example of acceptable writing.
    B. The words *more fast* should be changed to *faster*.
    C. There should be a comma after the words *desktop computer*.
    D. The word *than* should be changed to *then*.

    17._____

18. The typist used an extention cord in order to connect her typewriter to the outlet nearest to her desks.
    A. This is an example of acceptable writing.
    B. A period should be placed after the word *cord*, and the word *in* should have a capital *I*.
    C. A comma should be placed after the word *typewriter*.
    D. The word *extention* should be spelled *extension*.

    18.____

19. He would have went to the conference if he had received an invitation.
    A. This is an example of acceptable writing.
    B. The word *went* should be replaced by the word *gone*.
    C. The word *had* should be replaced by *would have*.
    D. The word *conference* should be spelled *conferance*.

    19.____

20. In order to make the report neater, he spent many hours rewriting it.
    A. This is an example of acceptable writing.
    B. The word *more* should be inserted before the word *neater*.
    C. There should be a colon after the word *neater*.
    D. The word *spent* should be changed to *have spent*.

    20.____

21. His supervisor told him that he should of read the memorandum more carefully.
    A. This is an example of acceptable writing.
    B. The word *memorandum* should be spelled *memorandom*.
    C. The word *of* should be replaced by the word *have*.
    D. The word *carefully* should be replaced by the word *careful*.

    21.____

22. It was decided that two separate reports should be written.
    A. This is an example of acceptable writing.
    B. A comma should be inserted after the word *decided*.
    C. The word *be* should be replaced by the word *been*.
    D. A colon should be inserted after the word *that*.

    22.____

23. She don't seem to understand that the work must be done as soon as possible.
    A. This is an example of acceptable writing.
    B. The word *doesn't* should replace the word *don't*.
    C. The word *why* should replace the word *that*.
    D. The word *as* before the word *soon* should be eliminated.

    23.____

24. He excepted praise from his supervisor for a job well done.
    A. This is an example of acceptable writing.
    B. The word *excepted* should be spelled *accepted*.
    C. The order of the words *well done* should be changed to *done well*.
    D. There should be a comma after the word *supervisor*.

    24.____

25. What appears to be intentional errors in grammar occur several times in the passage.
    A. This is an example of acceptable writing.
    B. The word *occur* should be spelled *occur*.
    C. The word *appears* should be changed to *appear*.
    D. The phrase *several times* should be changed to *from time to time*.

25.____

KEY (CORRECT ANSWERS)

1.	C	11.	B
2.	C	12.	C
3.	D	13.	D
4.	A	14.	A
5.	C	15.	B
6.	A	16.	A
7.	B	17.	B
8.	A	18.	D
9.	D	19.	B
10.	D	20.	A

21.	C
22.	A
23.	B
24.	B
25.	C

TEST 2

DIRECTIONS: Each question consists of a sentence which may or may not be an example of good formal English usage. Examine each sentence, considering grammar, punctuation, spelling, capitalization, and awkwardness. Then choose the CORRECT statement about it from the four options below it. If the English usage in the sentence given is better than any of the changes suggested in options B, C, or D, pick option A. Do not pick an option that will change the meaning of the sentence. *PRINT THE LETTER OF THE CORRECT ANSWER IN THE SPACE AT THE RIGHT.*

1. I don't know who could possibly of broken it. 1.____
   A. This is an example of acceptable writing.
   B. The word *who* should be replaced by the word *whom*.
   C. The word *of* should be replaced by the word *have*.
   D. The word *broken* should be replaced by the word *broke*.

2. Telephoning is easier than to write. 2.____
   A. This is an example of acceptable writing.
   B. The word *telephoning* should be spelled *telephoneing*.
   C. The word *than* should be replaced by the word *then*.
   D. The words *to write* should be replaced by the word *writing*.

3. The two operators who have been assigned to these consoles are on vacation. 3.____
   A. This is an example of acceptable writing.
   B. A comma should be placed after the word *operators*.
   C. The word *who* should be replaced by the word *whom*.
   D. The word *are* should be replaced by the word *is*.

4. You were suppose to teach me how to operate a plugboard. 4.____
   A. This is an example of acceptable writing,
   B. The word *were* should be replaced by the word *was*.
   C. The word *suppose* should be replaced by the word *supposed*.
   D. The word *teach* should be replaced by the word *team*.

5. If you had taken my advice; you would have spoken with him. 5.____
   A. This is an example of acceptable writing.
   B. The word *advice* should be spelled *advise*.
   C. The words *had taken* should be replaced by the word *take*.
   D. The semicolon should be changed to a comma.

6. The clerk could have completed the assignment on time if he knows where these materials were located. 6.____
   A. This is an example of acceptable writing.
   B. The word *knows* should be replaced by *had known*.
   C. The word "were" should be replaced by *had been*.
   D. The words *where these materials were located* should be replaced by *the location of these materials*.

7. All employees should be given safety training. Not just those who have accidents.
   A. This is an example of acceptable writing,
   B. The period after the word *training* should be changed to a colon.
   C. The period after the word *training* should be changed to a semicolon, and the first letter of the word *Not* should be changed to a small *n*.
   D. The period after the word *training* should be changed to a comma, and the first letter of the word *Not* should be changed to a small *n*,

8. This proposal is designed to promote employee awareness of the suggestion program, to encourage employee participation in the program, and to increase the number of suggestions submitted.
   A. This is an example of acceptable writing.
   B. The word *proposal* should be spelled *proposal*.
   C. The words *to increase the number of suggestions submitted* should be changed to *an increase in the number of suggestions is expected*.
   D. The word *promote* should be changed to *enhance*, and the word *increase* should be changed to *add to*.

9. The introduction of inovative managerial techniques should be preceded by careful analysis of the specific circumstances and conditions in each department.
   A. This is an example of acceptable writing.
   B. The word *techniques* should be spelled *techneques*.
   C. The word *inovative* should be spelled *innovative*.
   D. A comma should be placed after the word *circumstances* and after the word *conditions*.

10. This occurrence indicates that such criticism embarrasses him.
    A. This is an example of acceptable writing.
    B. The word *occurrence* should be spelled *occurrence*.
    C. The word *criticism* should be spelled *creticism*.
    D. The word *embarrasses* should be spelled *embarasses*.

11. He can recommend a mechanic whose work is reliable.
    A. This is an example of acceptable writing.
    B. the word *reliable* should be spelled *relyable*.
    C. The word *whose* should be spelled *who's*.
    D. The word *mechanic* should be spelled *mecanic*.

12. She typed quickly; like someone who had not a moment to lose.
    A. This is an example of acceptable writing.
    B. The word *not* should be removed.
    C. The semicolon should be changed to a comma.
    D. The word *quickly* should be placed before instead of after the word *typed*.

13. She insisted that she had to much work to do. 13._____
    A. This is an example of acceptable writing.
    B. The word *insisted* should be spelled *insisted*.
    C. The word *to* used in front of *much* should be spelled *too*.
    D. The word *do* should be changed to *be done*.

14. The report, along with the accompanying documents, were submitted for review. 14._____
    A. This is an example of acceptable writing.
    B. The words *were submitted* should be changed to *was submitted*.
    C. The word *accompanying* should be spelled *accompaning*.
    D. The comma after the word *report* should be taken out.

15. If others must use your files, be certain that they understand how the system works, but insist that you do all the filing and refiling. 15._____
    A. This is an example of acceptable writing.
    B. There should be a period after the word *works*, and the word *but* should start a new sentence.
    C. The words *filing* and *refiling* should be spelled *fileing* and *refileing*.
    D. There should be a comma after the word *but*.

16. The appeal was not considered because of its late arrival. 16._____
    A. This is an example of acceptable writing.
    B. The word *its* should be changed to *it's*.
    C. The word *its* should be changed to *the*.
    D. The words *late arrival* should be changed to *arrival late*.

17. The letter must be read carefully to determine under which subject it should be filed. 17._____
    A. This is an example of acceptable writing.
    B. The word *under* should be changed to *at*.
    C. The word *determine* should be spelled *determin*.
    D. The word *carefully* should be spelled *carefuly*.

18. He showed potential as an office manager, but he lacked skill in delegating work. 18._____
    A. This is an example of acceptable writing.
    B. The word *delegating* should be spelled *delagating*.
    C. The word *potential* should be spelled *potencial*.
    D. The words *he lacked* should be changed to *was lacking*.

19. His supervisor told him that it would be all right to receive personal mail at the office. 19._____
    A. This is an example of acceptable writing.
    B. The words *all right* should be changed to *alright*.
    C. The word *personal* should be spelled *personel*.
    D. The word *mail* should be changed to *letters*.

20. The report, along with the accompanying documents, were submitted for review.   20._____
    A. This is an example of acceptable writing.
    B. The words *were submitted* should be changed to *was submitted*.
    C. The word *accompanying* should be spelled *accompaning*.
    D. The comma after the word *report* should be taken out.

KEY (CORRECT ANSWERS)

1.	C	11.	A
2.	D	12.	C
3.	A	13.	C
4.	C	14.	B
5.	D	15.	A
6.	B	16.	A
7.	D	17.	D
8.	A	18.	A
9.	C	19.	A
10.	A	20.	B

BASIC FUNDAMENTALS OF A FINANCIAL STATEMENT

TABLE OF CONTENTS

	PAGE
Commentary	1
Financial Reports	1
Balance Sheet	1
Assets	1
The ABC Manufacturing Co., Inc.	
Consolidated Balance Sheet – December 31	2
Fixed Assets	3
Depreciation	4
Intangibles	4
Liabilities	5
Reserves	6
Capital Stock	6
Surplus	6
What Does the Balance Sheet Show?	7
Net Working Capital	7
Inventory and Inventory Turnover	8
Net Book Value of Securities	8
Proportion of Bonds, Preferred and Common Stock	9
The Income Account	10
Cost of Sales	11
The ABC Manufacturing Co., Inc.	
Consolidated Income and Earned Surplus – December 31	11
Maintenance	12
Interest Charges	13
Net Income	13
Analyzing the Income Account	14
Interest Coverage	15
Earnings Per Common Share	15
Stock Prices	16
Important Terms and Concepts	17

BASIC FUNDAMENTALS OF A FINANCIAL STATEMENT

COMMENTARY

The ability to read and understand a financial statement is a basic requirement for the accountant, auditor, account clerk, bookkeeper, bank examiner, budget examiner, and, of course, for the executive who must manage and administer departmental affairs.

FINANCIAL REPORTS

Are financial reports really as difficult as all that? Well, if you know they are not so difficult because you have worked with them before, this section will be of auxiliary help for you. However, if you find financial statements a bit murky, but realize their great importance to you, we ought to get along fine together. For "mathematics," all we'll use is fourth-grade arithmetic.

Accountants, like all other professionals, have developed a specialized vocabulary. Sometimes this is helpful and sometimes plain confusing (like their practice of calling the income account, "Statement of Profit and Loss," when it is bound to be one or the other). But there are really only a score or so technical terms that you will have to get straight in mind. After that is done, the whole foggy business will begin to clear and in no time at all you'll be able to talk as wisely as the next fellow.

BALANCE SHEET

Look at the sample balance sheet printed on Page 2, and we'll have an insight into how it is put together. This particular report is neither the simplest that could be issued, nor the most complicated. It is a good average sample of the kind of report issues by an up-to-date manufacturing company.

Note particularly that the balance sheet represents the situation as it stood on one particular day, December 31, not the record of a year's operation. This balance sheet is broken into two parts on the left are shown *ASSETS* and on the right *LIABILITIES*. Under the asset column, you will find listed the value of things the company owns or are owed to the company. Under liabilities are listed the things the company owes to others, plus reserves, surplus, and the stated value of the stockholders' interest in the company.

One frequently hears the comment, "Well, I don't see what a good balance sheet is anyway, because the assets and liabilities are always the same whether the company is successful or not."

It is true that they always balance and, by itself, a balance sheet doesn't tell much until it is analyzed. Fortunately, we can make a balance sheet tell its story without too much effort—often an extremely revealing story, particularly, if we compare the records of several years.

ASSETS

The first notation on the asset side of the balance sheet is *CURRENT ASSETS* (Item 1). In general, current assets include cash and things that can be turned into cash in a hurry, or that, in the normal course of business, will be turned into cash in the reasonably near future, usually within a year.

Item 2 on our sample sheet is *CASH*. Cash is just what you would expect—bills and silver in the till and money on deposit in the bank.

UNITED STATES GOVERNMENT SECURITIES is Item 3. The general practice is to show securities listed as current assets at cost or market value, whichever is lower. The figure, for all reasonable purposes, represents the amount by which total cash could be easily increased if the company wanted to sell these securities.

The next entry is *ACCOUNTS RECEIVABLE* (Item 4). Here we find the total amount of money owed to the company by its regular business creditors and collectable within the next year. Most of the money is owed to the company by its customers for goods that the company delivered on credit. If this were a department store instead of a manufacturer, what you owed the store on our charge account would be included here. Because some people fail to pay their bills, the company sets up a reserve for doubtful accounts, which it subtracts from all the money owed.

THE ABC MANUFACTURING COMPANY, INC.
CONSOLIDATED BALANCE SHEET – DECEMBER 31

Item			Item		
1. CURRENT ASSETS			16. CURRENT LIABILITIES		
2. Cash			17. Accts. Payable		$300,000
3. U.S. Government Securities			18. Accrued Taxes		800,000
4. Accounts Receivable (less reserves)		2,000,000	19. Accrued Wages, interest and Other Expenses		370,000
5. Inventories (at lower of cost or market)		2,000,000	20. Total Current Liabilities		$1,470,000
6. Total Current Assets		$7,000,000	21. FIRST MORTGAGE SINKING FUND BONDS, 3½ % DUE 2020		$2,000,000
7. INVESTMENT IN AFFILIATED COMPANY Not consolidated (at cost, not in excess of net assets)		200,000	22. RESERVE FOR CONTINGENCIES		200,000
8. OTHER INVESTMENTS At cost, less than market		100,000	23. CAPITAL STOCK: 24. 5% Preferred Stock (authorized and issued 10,000 shares of $100 par shares of $100 (par value)	$1,000,000	
9. PLANT IMPROVEMENT FUND		550,000			
10. PROPERTY, PLANT AND EQUIPMENT: Cost	$8,000,000		25. Common stock (authorized and issued 400,000 shares of no par value)	1,000,000	
11. Less Reserve for Depreciation	5,000,000				2,000,000
12. NET PROPERTY		3,000,000	26. SURPLUS:		
13. PREPAYMENTS		50,000	27. Earned	3,530,000	
14. DEFERRED CHARGES		100,000	28. Capital (arising from sale of common capital stock at price in excess of stated value)	1,900,000	
15. PATENTS AND GOODWILL		100,000			
					5,430,000
TOTAL		$11,000,000	TOTAL		$11,100,000

Item 5, *INVENTORIES*, is the value the company places on the supplies it owns. The inventory of a manufacturer may contain raw materials that it uses in making the things it sells, partially finished goods in process of manufacture, and, finally, completed merchandise that it is ready to sell. Several methods are used to arrive at the value placed on these various items. The most common is to value them at their cost or present market value, whichever is lower.

You can be reasonably confident, however, that the figure given is an honest and significant one for the particular industry if the report is certified by a reputable firm of public accountants.

Next on the asset side is *TOTAL CURRENT ASSETS* (Item 6). This is an extremely important figure when used in connection with other items in the report, which we will come to presently. Then we will discover how to make total current assets tell their story.

INVESTMENT IN AFFILIATED COMPANY Item 7) represents the cost to our parent company of the capital stock of its subsidiary or affiliated company. A subsidiary is simply one company that is controlled by another. Most corporations that own other companies outright lump the figures in a CONSOLIDATED BALANCE SHEET. This means that, under cash, for example, one would find a total figure that represented all of the cash of the parent company and of its wholly owned subsidiary. This is a perfectly reasonable procedure because, in the last analysis, all of the money is controlled by the same persons.

Our typical company shows that it has *OTHER INVESTMENTS* (Item 8), in addition to its affiliated company. Sometimes good marketable securities other than Government bonds are carried as current assets, but the more conservative practice is to list these other security holdings separately. If they have been bought as a permanent investment, they would always be shown by themselves. "At cost, less than market" means that our company paid $100,000 for these other investments, but they are now worth more.

Among our assets is a *PLANT IMPROVEMENT FUND* (Item 9). Of course, this item does not appear in all company balance sheets, but is typical of special funds that companies set up for one purpose or another. For example, money set aside to pay off part of the bonded debt of a company might be segregated into a special fund. The money our directors have put aside to improve the plant would often be invested in Government bonds,

FIXED ASSETS

The next item (10) is *PROPERTY, PLANT, AND EQUIPMENT*, but it might just as well be labeled Fixed Assets as these items are used more or less interchangeably, Under Item 10, the report gives the value of land, buildings, and machinery and such movable things as trucks, furniture, and hand tools. Historically, probably more sins were committed against this balance sheet item than any other.

In olden days, cattlemen used to drive their stock to market in the city. It was a common trick to stop outside of town, spread out some salt for the cattle to make them thirsty and then let them drink all the water they could hold. When they were weighed for sale, the cattlemen would collect cash for the water the stock had drunk. Business buccaneers, taking the cue from their farmer friends, would often "write up" the value of their fixed assets. In other words, they would increase the value shown on the balance sheet, making the capital stock appear to be worth a lot more than it was. *Watered stock* proved a bad investment for most stockholders. The practice has, fortunately, been stopped, though it took major financial reorganizations to squeeze the water out of some securities.

The most common practice today is to list fixed assets at cost. Often, there is no ready market for most of the things that fall under this heading, so it is not possible to give market value. A good report will tell what is included under fixed assets and how it has been valued. If the value has been increased by *write-up* or decreased by *write-down*, a footnote explanation is usually given. A *write-up* might occur, for instance, if the value of real estate increased substantially. A *write-down* might follow the invention of a new machine that put an important part of the company's equipment out of date.

DEPRECIATION

Naturally, all of the fixed property of a company will wear out in time (except, of course, non-agricultural land). In recognition of this fact, companies set up a RESERVE FOR APPRECIATION (Item 11). If a truck costs $4,000 and is expected to last four years, it will be depreciated at the rate of $1,000 a year.

Two other items also frequently occur in connection with depreciation—*depletion* and *obsolescence*. Companies may lump depreciation, depletion, and obsolescence under a single title, or list them separately.

Depletion is a term used primarily by mining and oil companies (or any of the so-called extractive industries). Depletion means exhaust or use up. As the oil or other natural resource is used up, a reserve is set up, to compensate for the natural wealth the company no longer owns. This reserve is set up in recognition of the fact that, as the company sells its natural product, it must get back not only the cost of extracting but also the original cost of the natural resource.

Obsolescence represents the loss in value because a piece of property has gone out of date before it wore out. Airplanes are modern examples of assets that tend to get behind the times long before the parts wear out. (Women and husbands will be familiar with the speed at which ladies' hats "obsolesce.")

In our sample balance sheet we have placed the reserve for depreciation under fixed assets and then subtracted, giving us NET PROPERTY (Item 12), which we add into the asset column. Sometimes, companies put the reserve for depreciation in the liability column. As you can see, the effect is just the same whether it is *subtracted* from assets or *added* to liabilities.

The manufacturer, whose balance sheet we use, rents a New York showroom and pays his rent yearly, in advance. Consequently, he has listed under assets PREPAYMENTS (Item 13). This is listed as an asset because he has paid for the use of the showroom, but has not yet received the benefit from its use. The use is something coming to the firm in the following year and, hence, is an asset. The dollar value of this asset will decrease by one-twelfth each month during the coming year.

DEFERRED CHARGES (Item 14) represents a type of expenditure similar to prepayment. For example, our manufacturer brought out a new product last year, spending $100,000 introducing it to the market. As the benefit from this expenditure will be returned over months or even years to come, the manufacturer did not think it reasonable to charge the full expenditure against costs during the year. He has *deferred* the charges and will write them off gradually.

INTANGIBLES

The last entry in our asset column is PATENTS AND GOODWILL (Item 15). If our company were a young one, set up to manufacturer some new patented product, it would probably carry its patents at a substantial figure. In fact, *intangibles* of both old and new companies are often of great but generally unmeasurable worth.

Company practice varies considerably in assigning value to intangibles. Proctor & Gamble, despite the tremendous goodwill that has been built up for *Ivory Soap*, has reduced all of its intangibles to the nominal $1. Some of the big cigarette companies, on the contrary, place a high dollar value on the goodwill their brand names enjoy. Companies that spend a good deal for research and the development of new products are more inclined than others to reflect this fact in the value assigned to patents, license agreements, etc.

LIABILITIES

The liability side of the balance sheet appears a little deceptive at first glance. Several of the entries simply don't sound like liabilities by any ordinary definition of the term.

The first term on the liability side of any balance sheet is usually *CURRENT LIABILITIES* (Item 16). This is a companion to the Current Assets item across the page and includes all debts that fall due within the next year. The relation between current assets and current liabilities is one of the most revealing things to be gotten from the balance sheet, but we will go into that quite thoroughly later on.

ACCOUNTS PAYABLE (Item 17) represents the money that the company owes to its ordinary business creditors—unpaid bills for materials, supplies, insurance, and the like. Many companies itemize the money they owe in a much more detailed fashion than we have done, but, as you will see, the totals are the most interesting thing to us.

Item 18, *ACCRUED TAXES*, is the tax bill that the company estimates it still owes for the past year. We have lumped all taxes in our balance sheet, as many companies do. However, sometimes you will find each type of tax given separately. If the detailed procedure is followed, the description of the tax is usually quite sufficient to identify the separate items.

Accounts Payable was defined as the money the company owed to its regular business creditors. The company also owes, on any given day, wages to its own employees; interest to its bondholders and to banks from which it may have borrowed money; fees to its attorneys; pensions, etc. These are all totaled under *ACCRUED WAGES, INTEREST AND OTHER EXPENSES* (Item 19).

TOTAL CURRENT LIABILITIES (Item 20) is just the sum of everything that the company owed on December 31 and which must be paid sometime in the next twelve months.

It is quite clear that all of the things discussed above are liabilities. The rest of the entries on the liability side of the balance sheet, however, do not seem at first glance to be liabilities.

Our balance sheet shows that the company, on December 31, had $2,000,000 of 3½ percent First Mortgage BONDS outstanding (Item 21). Legally, the money received by a company when it sells bonds is considered a loan to the company. Therefore, it is obvious that the company owes to the bondholders an amount equal to the face value or the *call price* of the bonds it has outstanding. The call price is a figure usually larger than the face value of the bonds at which price the company can *call* the bonds in from the bondholders and pay them off before they ordinarily fall due. The date that often occurs as part of the name of a bond is the date at which the company has promised to pay off the loan from the bondholders.

RESERVES

The next heading, *RESERVE FOR CONTINGENCIES* (Item 22) sounds more like an asset than a liability. "My reserves," you might say, "are dollars in the bank, and dollars in the bank are assets.

No one would deny that you have something there. In fact, the corporation treasurer also has his reserve for contingencies balanced by either cash or some kind of unspecified investment on the asset side of the ledger. His reason for setting up a reserve on the liability side of the balance sheet is a precaution against making his financial position seem better than it is. He decided that the company might have to pay out this money during the coming year if certain things happened. If he did not set up the "reserve," his surplus would appear larger by an amount equal to his reserve.

A very large reserve for contingencies or a sharp increase in this figure from the previous year should be examined closely by the investor. Often, in the past, companies tried to hide their true earnings by transferring funds into a contingency reserve. As a reserve looks somewhat like a true liability, stockholders were confused about the real value of their securities. When a reserve is not set up for protection against some very probable loss or expenditure, it should be considered by the investor as part of surplus.

CAPITAL STOCK

Below reserves there is a major heading, CAPITAL STOCK (Item 23). Companies may have one type of security outstanding, or they may have a dozen. All of the issues that represent shares of ownership are capital, regardless of what they are called on the balance sheet—preferred stock, preference stock, common stock, founders' shares, capital stock, or something else.

Our typical company has one issue of 5 percent PREFERRED STOCK (Item 24). It is called *preferred* because those who own it have a right to dividends and assets before the *common* stockholders—that is, the holders are in a preferred position as owners. Usually, preferred stockholders do not have a voice in company affairs unless the company fails to pay them dividends at the promised rate. Their rights to dividends are almost always *cumulative*. This simply means that all past dividends must be paid before the other stockholders can receive anything. Preferred stockholders are not creditors of the company so it cannot properly be said that the company *owes* them the value of their holdings. However, in case the company decided to go out of business, preferred stockholders would have a prior claim on anything that was left in the company treasury after all of the creditors, including the bondholders, were paid off. In practice, this right does not always mean much, but it does explain why the book value of their holdings is carried as a liability.

COMMON STOCK (Item 25) is simple enough as far as definition is concerned. It represents the rights of the ordinary owner of the company. Each company has as many owners as it has stockholders. The proportion of the company that each stockholder owns is determined by the number of shares he has. However, neither the book value of a no-par common stock, nor the par value of an issue that has a given par, can be considered as representing either the original sale price, the market value, or what would be left for the stockholders if the company were liquidated.

A profitable company will seldom be dissolved. Once things have taken such a turn that dissolution appears desirable, the stated value of the stock is generally nothing but a fiction. Even if the company is profitable as a going institution, once it ceases to function even its tangible assets drop in value because there is not usually a ready market for its inventory of raw materials and semi-finished goods, or its plant and machinery.

SURPLUS

The last major heading on the liability side of the balance sheet is SURPLUS (Item 26). The surplus, of course, is not a liability in the popular sense at all. It represents, on our balance sheet, the difference between the stated value of our common stock and the net assets behind the stock.

Two different kinds of surplus frequently appear on company balance sheets, and our company has both kinds. The first type listed is EARNED surplus (Item 27). Earned surplus is roughly similar to your own savings. To the corporation, earned surplus is that part of net income which has not been paid to stockholders as dividends. It still belongs to you, but the directors have decided that it is best for the company and the stockholders to keep it in the business. The surplus may be invested in the plant just as you might invest part of your savings in your home. It may also be in cash or securities.

In addition to the earned surplus, our company also has a *CAPITAL* surplus (Item 28) of $1,900.00, which the balance sheet explains arose from selling the stock at a higher cost per share than is given as its stated value. A little arithmetic shows that the stock is carried on the books at $2.50 a share while the capital surplus amounts to $4.75 a share. From this we know that the company actually received an average of $7.25 net a share for the stock when it was sold.

WHAT DOES THE BALANCE SHEET SHOW?

Before we undertake to analyze the balance sheet figures, a word on just what an investor can expect to learn is in order. A generation or more ago, before present accounting standards had gained wide acceptance, considerable imagination went into the preparation of balance sheets. This, naturally, made the public skeptical of financial reports. Today, there is no substantial ground for skepticism. The certified public accountant, the listing requirements of the national stock exchanges, and the regulations of the Securities and Exchange Commission have, for all practical purposes, removed the grounds for doubting the good faith of financial reports.

The investor, however, is still faced with the task of determining the significance of the figures. As we have already seen, a number of items are based, to a large degree, upon estimates, while others are, of necessity, somewhat arbitrary.

NET WORKING CAPITAL

There is one very important thing that we can find from the balance sheet and accept with the full confidence that we know what we are dealing with. That is net working capital, sometimes simply called working capital.

On the asset side of our balance sheet, we have added up all of the current assets and show the total as Item 6. On the liability side, Item 20 gives the total of current liabilities. *Net working capital* or *net current assets* is the difference left after subtracting current liabilities from current assets. If you consider yourself an investor rather than a speculator, you should always insist that any company in which you invest have a comfortable amount of working capital. The ability of a company to meet its obligations with ease, expand its volume as business expands and take advantage of opportunities as they present themselves, is, to an important degree, determined by its working capital.

Probably the question in your mind is: "*Just what does 'comfortable amount' of working capital mean?*" Well, there are several methods used by analysts to judge whether a particular company has a sound working capital position. The first rough test for an industrial company is to compare the working capital figure with the current liability total. Most analysts say that minimum safety requires that net working capital at least equal current liabilities. Or, put another way, current assets should be at least twice as large as current liabilities.

There are so many different kinds of companies, however, that this test requires a great deal of modification if it is to be really helpful in analyzing companies in different industries. To help you interpret the current position of a company in which you are considering investing, the *current ratio* is more helpful than the dollar total of working capital. The current ratio is current assets divided by current liabilities.

In addition to working capital and current ratio, there are two other ways of testing the adequacy of the current position. *Net quick assets* provide a rigorous and important test of a company's ability to meet its current obligations. Net quick assets are found by taking total current assets (Item 6) and subtracting the value of inventories (Item 5). A well-fixed industrial company should show a reasonable excess of quick assets over current liabilities.

Finally, many analysts say that a good industrial company should have at least as much working capital (current assets less current liabilities) as the total book value of its bonds and preferred stock. In other words, current liabilities, bonded debt, and preferred stock *altogether* should not exceed the current assets.

INVENTORY AND INVENTORY TURNOVER

In the recent past, there has been much talk of inventories. Many commentators have said that these carry a serious danger to company earnings if management allows them to increase too much. Of course, this has always been true, but present high prices have made everyone more inventory-conscious than usual.

There are several dangers in a large inventory position. In the first place, sharp drop in price may cause serious losses; also, a large inventory may indicate that the company has accumulated a big supply of unsalable merchandise. The question still remains, however: "What do we mean by large inventory?"

As you certainly realize, an inventory is large or small only in terms of the yearly turnover and the type of business. We can discover the annual turnover of our sample company by dividing inventories (Item 5) into total annual sales (item "a" on the income account).

It is also interesting to compare the value of the inventory of a company being studied with total current assets. Again, however, there is considerable variation between different types of companies, so that the relationship becomes significant only when compared with similar companies.

NET BOOK VALUE OF SECURITIES

There is one other very important thing that can be gotten from the balance sheet, and that is the net book or equity value of the company's securities. We can calculate the net book value of each of the three types of securities our company has outstanding by a little very simple arithmetic. *Book value* means *the value at which something is carried on the books of the company.*

The full rights of the bondholders come before any of the rights of the stockholders, so, to find the net book value or net tangible assets backing up the bonds we add together the balance sheet value of the bonds, preferred stock, common stock, reserve, and surplus. This gives us a total of $9,630,000, (We would not include contingency reserve if we were reasonably sure the contingency was going to arise, but, as general reserves are often equivalent to surplus, it is, usually, best to treat the reserve just as though it were surplus.) However, part of this value represents the goodwill and patents carried at $100,000, which is not a tangible item, so, to be conservative, we subtract this amount, leaving $9,530,000 as the total net book value of the bonds. This is equivalent to $4,765 for each $1,000 bond, a generous figure. To calculate the net book value of the preferred stock, we must eliminate the face value of the bonds, and then, following the same procedure, add the value of the preferred stock, common stock, reserve, and surplus, and subtract goodwill. This gives us a total net book value for the preferred stock of $7,530 or $753 for each share of $100 par value preferred. This is also very good coverage for the preferred stock, but we must examine current earnings before becoming too enthusiastic about the value of any security.

The net book value of the common stock, while an interesting figure, is not so important as the coverage on the senior securities. In case of liquidation, there is seldom much left for the common stockholders because of the normal loss in value of company assets when they are put up for sale, as mentioned before. The book value figure, however, does give us a basis for comparison with other companies. Comparisons of net book value over a period of years also show us if the company is a soundly growing one or, on the other hand, is losing ground. Earnings, however, are our important measure of common stock values, as we will see shortly.

The net book value of the common stock is found by adding the stated value of the common stock, reserves, and surplus and then subtracting patents and goodwill. This gives us a total net book value of $6,530,000. As there are 400,000 shares of common outstanding, each share has a net book value of $16.32. You must be careful not to be misled by book value figures, particularly of common stock. Profitable companies (Coca-Cola, for example) often show a very low net book value and very substantial earnings. Railroads, on the other hand, may show a high book value for their common stock but have such low or irregular earnings that the market price of the stock is much less than its apparent book value. Banks, insurance companies, and investment trusts are exceptions to what we have said about common stock net book value. As their assets are largely liquid (i.e., cash, accounts receivable, and marketable securities), the book value of their common stock sometimes indicates its value very accurately.

PROPORTION OF BONDS, PREFERRED AND COMMON STOCK

Before investing, you will want to know the proportion of each kind of security issued by the company you are considering. A high proportion of bonds reduces the attractiveness of both the preferred and common stock, while too large an amount of preferred detracts from the value of the common.

The *bond ratio* is found by dividing the face value of the bonds (Item 21), or $2,000,000, by the total value of the bonds, preferred stock, common stock, reserve, and surplus, or $9,630,000. This shows that bonds amount to about 20 percent of the total of bonds, capital, and surplus.

The *preferred stock ratio* is found in the same way, only we divide the stated value of the preferred stock by the total of the other five items. Since we have half as much preferred stock as we have bonds, the preferred ratio is roughly 10.

Naturally, the *common stock ratio* will be the difference between 100 percent and the totals of the bonds and preferred, or 70 percent in our sample company. You will want to remember that the most valuable method of determining the common stock ratio is in combination with reserve and surplus. The surplus, as we have noted, is additional backing for the common stock and usually represents either original funds paid in to the company in excess of the stated value of the common stock (capital surplus), or undistributed earnings (earned surplus).

Most investment analysts carefully examine industrial companies that have more than about a quarter of their capitalization represented by bonds, while common stock should total at least as much as all senior securities (bonds and preferred issues). When this is not the case, companies often find it difficult to raise new capital. Banks don't like to lend them money because of the already large debt, and it is sometimes difficult to sell common stock because of all the bond interest or preferred dividends that must be paid before anything is available for the common stockholder.

Railroads and public utility companies are exceptions to most of the rules of thumb that we use in discussing The ABC Manufacturing Company, Inc. Their situation is different because of the tremendous amounts of money they have invested in their fixed assets, their small inventories and he ease with which they can collect their receivables. Senior securities of railroads and utility companies frequently amount to more than half of their capitalization, Speculators often interest themselves in companies that have a high proportion of debt or preferred stock because of the *leverage factor*. A simple illustration will show why. Let us take, for example, a company with $10,000,000 of 4 percent bonds outstanding. If the company is earning $440,000 before bond interest, there will be only $40,000 left for the common stock ($10,000,000 at 4% equals $400,000). However, an increase of only 10 percent in earnings (to $484,000) will leave $84,000 for common stock dividends, or an increase of more than 100 percent. If there is only a small common issue, the increase in earnings per share would appear very impressive.

You have probably already noticed that a decline of 10 percent in earnings would not only wipe out everything available for the common stock, but result in the company being unable to cover its full interest on its bonds without dipping into surplus. This is the great danger of so-called high leverage stocks and also illustrates the fundamental weakness of companies that have a disproportionate amount of debt or preferred stock. Investors would do well to steer clear of them. Speculators, however, will continue to be fascinated by the market opportunities they offer.

THE INCOME ACCOUNT

The fundamental soundness of a company, as shown by its balance sheet, is important to investors, but of even greater interest is the record of its operation. Its financial structure shows much of its ability to weather storms and pick up speed when times are good. It is the income record, however, that shows us how a company is actually doing and gives us our best guide to the future.

The *Consolidated Income and Earned Surplus* account of our company is stated on the next page. Follow the items given there and we will find out just how our company earned its money, what it did with its earnings, and what it all means in terms of our three classes of securities. We have used a combined income and surplus account because it is the form most frequently followed by industrial companies. However, sometimes the two statements are given separately. Also, a variety of names are used to describe this same part of the financial report. Sometimes it is called profit and loss account, sometimes *record of earnings*, and, often, simply *income account*. They are all the same thing.

The details that you will find on different income statements also vary a great deal. Some companies show only eight or ten separate items, while others will give a page or more of closely spaced entries that break down each individual type of revenue or cost. We have tried to strike a balance between extremes; give the major items that are in most income statements, omitting details that are only interesting to the expert analyst.

The most important source of revenue always makes up the first item on the income statement. In our company, it is *Net Sales* (Item "a"). If it were a railroad or a utility instead of a manufacturer, this item would be called *gross revenues*. In any case, it represents the money paid into the company by its customers. Net sales are given to show that the figure represents the amount of money actually received after allowing for discounts and returned goods.

Net sales or gross revenues, you will note, is given before any kind of miscellaneous revenue that might have been received from investments, the sale of company property, tax refunds, or the like. A well-prepared income statement is always set up this way so that the stockholder can estimate the success of the company in fulfilling its major job of selling goods or service. If this were not so, you could not tell whether the company was really losing or making money on its operations, particularly over the last few years when tax rebates and other unusual things have often had great influence on final net income figures.

The ABC Manufacturing Company, Inc.
CONSOLIDATED INCOME AND EARNED SURPLUS
For the Year Ended December 31

Item		
a. Sales		$10,000,000
b. COST OF SALES, EXPENSES AND OTHER OPERATING CHARGES:		
c. Cost of Goods Sold	$7,000,000	
d. Selling, Administrative & Gen. Expenses	500,000	
e. Depreciation	200,000	
f. Maintenance and Repairs	400,000	
g. Taxes (Other than Federal Inc. Taxes)	300,000	
h. NET PROFIT FROM OPERATIONS		8,400,000
i. OTHER INCOME:		$1,600,000
j. Royalties and Dividends	$250,000	
k. Interest	25,000	
l. TOTAL		$1,875,000
m. INTEREST CHARGES:		
n. Interest on Funded Debt	$70,000	
o. Other Interest	20,000	90,000
p. NET INCOME BEFORE PROVISION FOR FED. INCOME TAXES		$1,785,000
q. PROVISION FOR FEDERAL INCOME TAXES		678,300
r. NET INCOME		$1,106,700
s. DIVIDENDS		
t. Preferred Stock - $5.00 Per Share	$50,000	
u. Common Stock - $1.00 Per Share	400,000	
v. PROVISION FOR CONTINGENCIES	200,000	650,000
w. BALANCE CARRIED TO EARNED SURPLUS		456,700
x. EARNED SURPLUS – JANUARY 1		3,073,000
y. EARNED SURPLUS – DECEMBER 31		$3,530,000

COST OF SALES

    A general heading, *Cost of Sales, Expenses, and Other Operating Charges* (Item "b") is characteristic of a manufacturing company, but a utility company or railroad would call all of these things *operating expenses*.

    The most important subdivision is *Cost of Goods Sold* (Item "c"). Included under cost of goods sold are all of the expenses that go directly into the manufacture of the products the company sells—raw materials, wages, freight, power, and rent. We have lumped these expenses together, as many companies do. Sometimes, however, you will find each item listed separately. Analyzing a detailed income account is a pretty technical operation and had best be left to the expert.

We have shown separately, opposite "d," the *Selling, Administrative and General Expenses* of the past year. Unfortunately, there is little uniformity among companies in their treatment of these important non-manufacturing costs. Our figure includes the expenses of management; that is, executive salaries and clerical costs; commissions and salaries paid to salesmen; advertising expenses, and the like.

Depreciation ("e") shows us the amount that the company transferred from income during the year to the depreciation reserve that we ran across before as Item "11" on the balance sheet (Page 2). Depreciation must be charged against income unless the company is going to live on its own fat, something that no company can do for long and stay out of bankruptcy.

MAINTENANCE

Maintenance and Repairs (Item "f") represents the money spent to keep the plant in good operating order. For example, the truck that we mentioned under depreciation must be kept running day by day. The cost of new tires, recharging the battery, painting and mechanical repairs are all maintenance costs. Despite this day-to-day work on the truck, the company must still provide for the time when it wears out—hence, the reserve for depreciation.

You can readily understand from your own experience the close connection between maintenance and depreciation. If you do not take good care of your own car, you will have to buy a new one sooner than you would had you maintained it well. Corporations face the same problem with all of their equipment. If they do not do a good job of maintenance, much more will have to be set aside for depreciation to replace the abused tools and property.

Taxes are always with us. A profitable company always pays at least two types of taxes. One group of taxes are paid without regard to profits, and include real estate taxes, excise taxes, social security, and the like (Item "g"). As these payments are a direct part of the cost of doing business, they must be included before we can determine the *Net Profit From Operations* (Item "h").

Net Profit From Operations (sometimes called *gross profit*) tells us what the company made from manufacturing and selling its products. It is an interesting figure to investors because it indicates how efficiently and successfully the company operates in its primary purpose as a creator of wealth. As a glance at the income account will tell you, there are still several other items to be deducted before the stockholder can hope to get anything. You can also easily imagine that for many companies these other items may spell the difference between profit and loss. For these reasons, we use net profit from operations as an indicator of progress in manufacturing and merchandising efficiency, not as a judge of the investment quality of securities.

Miscellaneous Income not connected with the major purpose of the company is generally listed after net profit from operations. There are quite a number of ways that corporations increase their income, including interest and dividends on securities they own, fees for special services performed, royalties on patents they allow others to use, and tax refunds. Our income statement shows *Other Income* as Item "i," under which is shown income from *Royalties* and *Dividends* (Item "j"), and as a separate entry, *Interest* (Item "k") which the company received from its bond investments. The *Total* of other income (Item "l") shows us how much The ABC Manufacturing Company received from so-called *outside activities*. Corporations with diversified interests often receive tremendous amounts of other income.

INTEREST CHARGES

There is one other class of expenses that must be deducted from our income before we can determine the base on which taxes are paid, and that is *Interest Charges* (Item "m"). As our company has $2,000,000 worth of 3 ½ percent bonds outstanding, it will pay *Interest on Funded Debt* of $70,000 (Item "n"). During the year, the company also borrowed money from the bank, on which it, of course, paid interest, shown as *Other Interest* (Item "o").

Net Income Before Provision for Federal Income Taxes ("Item "p") is an interesting figure for historical comparison. It shows us how profitable the company was in all of its various operations. A comparison of this entry over a period of years will enable you to see how well the company had been doing as a business institution before the government stepped in for its share of net earnings. Federal taxes have varied so much in recent years that earnings before taxes are often a real help in judging business progress.

A few paragraphs back we mentioned that a profitable corporation pays two general types of taxes. We have already discussed those that are paid without reference to profits. *Provision for Federal Income Taxes* (Item "q") is ordinarily figured on the total income of the company after normal business expenses, and so appears on our income account below these charges. Bond interest, for example, as it is payment on a loan, is deducted beforehand. Preferred and common stock dividends, which are profits that go to owners of the company, come after all charges and taxes.

NET INCOME

After we have deducted all of our expenses and income taxes from total income, we get *Net Income* (Item "r"). Net income is the most interesting figure of all to the investor. Net income is the amount available to pay dividends on the preferred and common stock. From the balance sheet, we have learned a good deal about the company's stability and soundness of structure; from net profit from operations, we judge whether the company is improving in industrial efficiency. Net income tells us whether the securities of the company are likely to be a profitable investment.

The figure given for a single year is not nearly all of the store, however. As we have noted before, the historical record is usually more important than the figure for any given year. This is just as true of net income as any other item. So many things change from year to year that care must be taken not to draw hasty conclusions. During the war, Excess Profits Taxes had a tremendous effect on the earnings of many companies. In the next few years, carryback tax credits allowed some companies to show a net profit despite the fact that they had operated at a loss. Even net income can be a misleading figure unless one examines it carefully. A rough and easy way of judging how sound a figure it is would be to compare it with previous years.

The investor in stocks has a vital interest in *Dividends* (Item "s"). The first dividend that our company must pay is that on its *Preferred Stock* (Item "t"). Some companies will even pay preferred dividends out of earned surplus accumulated in the past if the net income is not large enough, but such a company is skating on thin ice unless the situation is most unusual.

The directors of our company decided to pay dividends totaling ($400,000 on the *Common Stock*, or $1 a share (Item "u"). As we have noted before, the amount of dividends paid is not determined by net income, but by a decision of the stockholders' representatives—the company's directors. Common dividends, just like preferred dividends, can be paid out of surplus if there is little or no net income. Sometimes companies do this if they have a long history of regular payments and don't want to spoil the record because of some special temporary situation that caused them to lose money. This occurs even less frequently and is more dangerous than paying preferred dividends out of surplus.

It is much more common, on the contrary, to plough earnings back into the business—a phrase you frequently see on the financial pages and in company reports. The directors of our typical company have decided to pay only $1 on the common stock, though net income would have permitted them to pay much more. They decided that the company should save the difference.

The next entry on our income account, *Provision for Contingencies* (Item "v") shows us where our reserve for contingencies arose. The treasurer of our typical company has put the provision for contingencies after dividends. However, you will discover, if you look at very many financial reports, that it is sometimes placed above net income.

All of the net income that was not paid out as dividends, or set aside for contingencies, is shown as *Balance Carried to Earned Surplus* (Item "w"). In other words, it is kept in the business. In previous years, the company had also earned more than it paid out so it had already accumulated by the beginning of the year an earned surplus of $3,073,000 (Item "x"). When we total the earned surplus accumulated during the year to that which the company had at the first of the year, we get the total earned surplus at the end of the year (Item "y"). You will notice that the total here is the same as that which we ran across on the balance sheet as Item 27.

Not all companies combine their income and surplus account. When they do not, you will find that *balance carried to surplus* will be the last item on the income account. The statement of consolidated surplus would appear as a third section of the corporation's financial report. A separate surplus account might be used if the company shifted funds for reserves to surplus during the year or made any other major changes in its method of treating the surplus account.

ANALYZING THE INCOME ACCOUNT

The income account, like the balance sheet, will tell us a lot more if we make a few detailed comparisons. The size of the totals on an income account doesn't mean much by itself. A company can have hundreds of millions of dollars in net sales and be a very bad investment. On the other hand, even a very modest profit in round figure may make a security attractive if there are only a small number of shares outstanding.

Before you select a company for investment, you will want to know something of its *margin of profit*, and how this figure has changed over the years. Finding the margin of profit is very simple. We just divide the net profit from operations (Item "h") by net sales (Item "a"). The figure we get (0.16) shows us that the company made a profit of 16 percent from operations. By itself, though, this is not very helpful. We can make it significant in two ways.

In the first place, we can compare it with the margin of profit in previous years, and, from this comparison, learn if the company excels other companies that do a similar type of business. If the margin of profit of our company is very low in comparison with other companies in the same field, it is an unhealthy sign. Naturally, if it is high, we have grounds to be optimistic.

Analysts also frequently use *operating ratio* for the same purpose. The operating ratio is the complement of the margin of profit. The margin of profit of our typical company is 16. The operating ratio is 84. You can find the operating ratio either by subtracting the margin of profit from 100 or dividing the total of operating costs ($8,400,000) by net sales ($10,000,000).

The margin of profit figure and the operating ratio, like all of those ratios we examined in connection with the balance sheet, give us general information about the company, help us judge its prospects for the future. All of these comparisons have significance for the long term as they tell us about the fundamental economic condition of the company. But you still have the right to ask: "Are the securities good investments for me now?"

Investors, as opposed to speculators, are primarily interested in two things. The first is safety for their capital and the second, regularity of income. They are also interested in the rate of return on their investment but, as you will see, the rate of return will be affected by the importance placed on safety and regularity. High income implies risk. Safety must be bought by accepting a lower return.

The safety of any security is determined primarily by the earnings of the company that are available to pay interest or dividends on the particular issues. Again, though, round dollar figures aren't of much help to us. What we want to know is the relationship between the total money available and the requirements for each of the securities issued by the company.

INTEREST COVERAGE

As the bonds of our company represent part of its debt, the first thing we want to know is how easily the company can pay the interest. From the income account we see that the company had total income of $1,875,000 (Item "1"). The interest charge on our bonds each year is $70,000 (3½ percent of $2,000,000—Item 21 on the balance sheet). Dividing total income by bond interest charges ($1,875,000 by $70,000) shows us that the company earned its bond interest 26 times over. Even after income taxes, bond interest was earned 17 times, a method of testing employed by conservative analysts. Before an industrial bond should be considered a safe investment, so our company has a wide margin of safety.

To calculate the *preferred dividend coverage* (i.e., the number of times preferred dividends were earned), we must use net income as our base, as Federal Income Taxes and all interest charges must be paid before anything is available for stockholders. As we have 10,000 shares of $100 par value of preferred stock which pays a dividend of 5 percent, the total dividend requirement for the preferred stock is $50,000 (Items 24 on the balance sheet and "t" on the income account).

EARNINGS PER COMMON SHARE

The buyer of common stocks is often more concerned with the earnings per share of his stock than he is with the dividend. It is usually earnings per share or, rather, prospective earnings per share, that influence stock market prices. Our income account does not show the earnings available for the common stock, so we must calculate it ourselves. It is net income less preferred dividends (Items "r"- "t"), or $1,056,700. From the balance sheet, we know that there are 400,000 shares outstanding, so the company earned about $2.64 per share.

All of these ratios have been calculated for a single year. It cannot be emphasized too strongly, however, that the record is more important to the investor than the report of any single year. By all the tests we have employed, both the bonds and the preferred stock of our typical company appear to be very good investments, if their market prices were not too high. The investor would want to look back, however, to determine whether the operations were reasonably typical of the company.

Bonds and preferred stocks that are very safe usually sell at pretty high prices, so the yield to the investor is small. For example, if our company has been showing about the same coverage on its preferred dividends for many years and there is good reason to believe that the future will be equally kind, the company would probably replace the old 5 percent preferred with a new issue paying a lower rate, perhaps 4 percent.

STOCK PRICES

As the common stock does not receive a guaranteed dividend, its market value is determined by a great variety of influences in addition to the present yield of the stock measured by its dividends. The stock market, by bringing together buyers and sellers from all over the world, reflects their composite judgment of the present and future value of the stock. We cannot attempt here to write a treatise on the stock market. There is one important ratio, however, that every common stock buyer considers. That is the ratio of earnings to market price.

The so-called *price-earnings ratio* is simply the earnings per share on the common stock divided into the market price. Our typical company earned $2.64 a common share in the year. If the stock were selling at $30 a share, its price-earnings ratio would be about 11.4. This is the basis figure that you would want to use in comparing the common stock of this particular company with other similar stocks.

17
IMPORTANT TERMS AND CONCEPTS

LIABILITIES
  WHAT THE COMPANY OWES—+ RESERVES + SURPLUS + STOCKHOLDERS INTEREST IN THE COMPANY

ASSETS
  WHAT THE COMPANY OWNS— + WHAT IS OWED TO THE COMPANY

FIXED ASSETS
  MACHINERY, EQUIPMENT, BUILDINGS, ETC.

EXAMPLES OF FIXED ASSETS
  DESKS, TABLES, FILING CABINETS, BUILDINGS, LAND, TIMBERLAND, CARS AND TRUCKS, LOCOMOTIVES AND FREIGHT CARS, SHIPYARDS, OIL LANDS, ORE DEPOSITS, FOUNDRIES

EXAMPLES OF:
  PREPAID EXPENSES
    PREPAID INSURANCE, PREPAID RENT, PREPAIDD ROYALTIES AND PREPAID INTEREST

  DEFERRED CHARGES
    AMORTIZATION OF BOND DISCOUNT, ORGANIZATION EXPENSE, MOVING EXPENSES, DEVELOPMENT EXPENSES

ACCOUNTS PAYABLE
  BILLS THE COMPANY OWES TO OTHERS

BONDHOLDERS ARE CREDITORS
  BOND CERTIFICATES ARE IOU'S ISSUED BY A COMPANY BACKED BY A PLEDGE

BONDHOLDERS ARE OWNERS
  A STOCK CERTIFICATE IS EVIDENCE OF THE SHAREHOLDER'S OWNERSHIP

EARNED SURPLUS
  INCOME PLOWED BACK INTO THE BUSINESS

NET SALES
  GROSS SALES MINUS DISCOUNTS AND RETURNED GOODS

NET INCOME
  = TOTAL INCOME MINUS ALL EXPENSES AND INCOME TAXES

www.ingramcontent.com/pod-product-compliance
Lightning Source LLC
Chambersburg PA
CBHW081822300426
44116CB00014B/2448